GMS INTENSIVE METHOD
Glossika Mass Sentences

Features: Sound files have A/B/C formats.

A Files	English - Target language 2x
B Files	English - space - Target 1x
C Files	Target language only 1x

Fea...
alg...
every day, with re...
for a total of 1000 sentences in 104 days.
Requires less than 20 minutes daily.

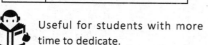
Useful for students with more
time to dedicate.

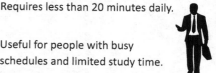
Useful for people with busy
schedules and limited study time.

HOW TO USE

❶ To familiarise yourself with IPA and spelling, Glossika recommends using the book while listening to A or C sound files and going through all 1000 sentences on your first day. Then you can start your training.

❷ Set up your schedule. It's your choice, you can choose 20, 50 or 100 sentences for daily practice. We recommend completing the following four steps.

Training Step **1**: Try repeating the sentences with the same speed and intonation in the A sound files.

Training Step **2**: Dictation: use the C sound files (and pausing) to write out each sentence (in script or IPA or your choice). Use the book to check your answers.

Training Step **3**: Recording: record the sentences as best you can. We recommend recording the same sentences over a 3-day period, and staggering them with new ones.

Training Step **4**: Use the B sound files to train your interpretation skills. Say your translation in the space provided.

❷ Set up your schedule. You can listen to a single GSR file daily or even double up. One book typically takes 3-4 months to complete.

❸ You can accompany with the GMS training when you have extra time to practice.

Reminder

Don't forget that if you run into problems, just skip over it! Keep working through the sentences all the way to the end and don't worry about the ones you don't get. You'll probably get it right the second time round. Remember, one practice session separated by *one* sleep session yields the best results!

Glossika Mass Sentences

French

Fluency 1

Complete Fluency Course

Michael Campbell

Maxime Paquin

Glossika

Glossika Mass Sentence Method

French Fluency 1

First published : NOV 2015
via license by Nolsen Bédon, Ltd.
Taipei, Taiwan

Authors: Michael Campbell, Maxime Paquin
Chief Editor: Michael Campbell
Translator: Michael Campbell, Maxime Paquin
Recording: Michael Campbell, Maxime Paquin
Editing Team: Claudia Chen, Sheena Chen
Consultant: Percy Wong
Programming: Edward Greve
Design: Glossika team

glossika.com

Glossika Series

The following languages are available (not all are published in English):

Afroasiatic

AM Amharic
ARE Egyptian Arabic
HA Hausa
IV Hebrew
AR Modern Standard Arabic
ARM Moroccan Arabic

Altaic

AZ Azerbaijani
JA Japanese
KK Kazakh
KR Korean
MN Mongolian
UZ Uzbek

Austroasiatic

KH Khmer
VNN Vietnamese (Northern)
VNS Vietnamese (Southern)

Austronesian

AMP Amis

TYS Atayal
BNN Bunun
ILO Ilokano
SDQ Seediq
TGL Tagalog
THW Thao

Caucasian

Dravidian

KAN Kannada
MAL Malayalam
TAM Tamil
TEL Telugu

IE: Baltic

LAV Latvian
LIT Lithuanian

IE: Celtic

CYM Welsh

IE: Germanic

EN American English
DA Danish
NL Dutch

DE German
IS Icelandic
NO Norwegian
SV Swedish

IE: Indo-Iranian

BEN Bengali
PRS Dari Persian
GUJ Gujarati
HI Hindi
KUR Kurmanji Kurdish
MAR Marathi
NEP Nepali
FA Persian
PAN Punjabi (India)
SIN Sinhala
KUS Sorani Kurdish
TGK Tajik
UR Urdu

IE: Other

SQ Albanian
HY Armenian
EU Basque
EO Esperanto
EL Greek

IE: Romance

PB Brazilian Portuguese
ES Castilian Spanish
CA Catalan
PT European Portuguese
FR French
IT Italian
ESM Mexican Spanish
RO Romanian

IE: Slavic

BEL Belarusian
BOS Bosnian
HR Croatian
CS Czech
MK Macedonian
PL Polish
RU Russian
SRP Serbian
SK Slovak
SL Slovene
UKR Ukrainian

Kartuli

KA Georgian

Niger-Congo

SW Swahili
YO Yoruba

Sino-Tibetan

MY Burmese
YUE Cantonese
ZH Chinese
HAK Hakka
ZS Mandarin Chinese (Beijing)
WUS Shanghainese
MNN Taiwanese
WUW Wenzhounese

Tai-Kadai

LO Lao
TH Thai

Uralic

EST Estonian
FI Finnish
HU Hungarian

Glossika Levels

Many of our languages are offered at different levels (check for availability):

Intro Level	Fluency Level	Expression Level
Pronunciation Courses	Fluency	Business Courses
Intro Course	Daily Life	Intensive Reading
	Travel	
	Business Intro	

Getting Started

For Busy People & Casual Learners

- 20 minutes per day, 3 months per book
- Use the Glossika Spaced Repetition (GSR) MP3 files, 1 per day. The files are numbered for you.
- Keep going and don't worry if you miss something on the first day, you will hear each sentence more than a dozen times over a 5 day period.

For Intensive Study

- 1-2 hours per day, 1 month per book

Log on to our website and download the Self Study Planner at: glossika.com/howto.

Steps:

1. Prepare (GMS-A). Follow the text as you listen to the GMS-A files (in 'GLOSSIKA-XX-GMS-A'). Listen to as many sentences as you can, and keep going even when you miss a sentence or two. Try to focus on the sounds and matching them to the text.
2. Listen (GMS-A). Try to repeat the target sentence with the speaker the second time you hear it.
3. Write (GMS-C). Write down the sentences as quickly as you can, but hit pause when you need to. Check your answers against the text.
4. Record (GMS-C). Listen to each sentence and record it yourself. Record from what you hear, not from reading the text. You can use your mobile phone or computer to do the recording. Play it back, and try to find the differences between the original and your recording.
5. Interpret (GMS-B). Try to recall the target sentence in the gap after you hear it in English. Try to say it out loud, and pause if necessary.

Glossika Mass Sentence Method

French

Fluency 1

This GMS Fluency Series accompanies the GMS recordings and is a supplementary course assisting you on your path to fluency. This course fills in the fluency training that is lacking from other courses. Instead of advancing in the language via grammar, GMS builds up sentences and lets students advance via the full range of expression required to function in the target language.

GMS recordings prepare the student through translation and interpretation to become proficient in speaking and listening.

Glossika Spaced Repetition (GSR) recordings are strongly recommended for those who have trouble remembering the content. Through the hundred days of GSR training, all the text in each of our GMS publications can be mastered with ease.

What is Glossika?

From the creation of various linguists and polyglots headed by Michael Campbell, Glossika is a comprehensive and effective system that delivers speaking and listening training to fluency.

It's wise to use Glossika training materials together with your other study materials. Don't bet everything on Glossika. Always use as many materials as you can get your hands on and do something from all of those materials daily. These are the methods used by some of the world's greatest polyglots and only ensures your success.

If you follow all the guidelines in our method you can also become proficiently literate as well. But remember it's easier to become literate in a language that you can already speak than one that you can't.

Most people will feel that since we only focus on speaking and listening, that the Glossika method is too tough. It's possible to finish one of our modules in one month, in fact this is the speed at which we've been training our students for years: 2 hours weekly for 4 weeks is all you need to complete one module. Our students are expected to do at least a half hour on their own every day through listening, dictation, and recording. If you follow the method, you will have completed 10,000 sentence repetitions by the end of the month. This is sufficient enough to start to feel your fluency come out, but you still have a long way to go.

This training model seems to fit well with students in East Asia learning tough languages like English, because they are driven by the fact that they need a better job or have some pressing issue to use their English. This drive makes them want to succeed.

Non-East Asian users of the Glossika Mass Sentence (GMS) methods are split in two groups: those who reap enormous benefit by completing the course, and others who give up because it's too tough to stick to the schedule. If you feel like our training is too overwhelming or demands too much of your time, then I suggest you get your hands on our Glossika Spaced Repetition (GSR) audio files which are designed for people like you. So if you're ambitious, use GMS. If you're too busy or can't stick to a schedule, use GSR.

Glossika Levels

The first goal we have in mind for you is Fluency. Our definition of fluency is simple and easy to attain: speaking full sentences in one breath. Once you achieve fluency, then we work with you on expanding your expression and vocabulary to all areas of language competency. Our three levels correlate to the European standard:

- Introduction = A Levels
- Fluency = B Levels
- Expression = C Levels

The majority of foreign language learners are satisfied at a B Level and a few continue on. But the level at which you want to speak a foreign language is your choice. There is no requirement to continue to the highest level, and most people never do as a B Level becomes their comfort zone.

Glossika Publications

Each Glossika publication comes in four formats:

- Print-On-Demand paperback text
- E-book text (available for various platforms)
- Glossika Mass Sentence audio files
- Glossika Spaced Repetition audio files

Some of our books include International Phonetic Alphabet (IPA) as well. Just check for the IPA mark on our covers.

We strive to provide as much phonetic detail as we can in our IPA transcriptions, but this is not always possible with every language.

As there are different ways to write IPA, our books will also let you know whether it's an underlying pronunciation (phonemic) with these symbols: / /, or if it's a surface pronunciation (phonetic) with these symbols: [ ].

IPA is the most scientific and precise way to represent the sounds of foreign languages. Including IPA in language training guides is taking a step away from previous decades of language publishing. We embrace the knowledge now available to everybody via online resources like Wikipedia which allow anybody to learn the IPA: something that could not be done before without attending university classes.

To get started, just point your browser to Wikipedia's IPA page to learn more about pronouncing the languages we publish.

4 Secrets of the Mass Sentence Method

When learning a foreign language it's best to use full sentences for a number of reasons:

1. Pronunciation—In languages like English, our words undergo a lot of pronunciation and intonation changes when words get strung together in sentences which has been well analyzed in linguistics. Likewise it is true with languages like Chinese where the pronunciations and tones from individual words change once they appear in a sentence. By following the intonation and prosody of a native speaker saying a whole sentence, it's much easier to learn rather than trying to say string each word together individually.

2. Syntax—the order of words, will be different than your own language. Human thought usually occurs in complete ideas. Every society has developed a way to express those ideas linearly by first saying what happened (the verb), or by first saying who did it (the agent), etc. Paying attention to this will accustom us to the way others speak.

3. Vocabulary—the meanings of words, never have just one meaning, and their usage is always different. You always have to learn words in context and which words they're paired with. These are called collocations. To "commit a crime" and to "commit to a relationship" use two different verbs in most other languages. Never assume that learning "commit" by itself will give you the answer. After a lifetime in lexicography, Patrick Hanks "reached the alarming conclusion that words don't have meaning," but rather that "definitions listed in dictionaries can be regarded as presenting meaning potentials rather than meanings as such." This is why collocations are so important.

4. Grammar—the changes or morphology in words are always in flux. Memorizing rules will not help you achieve fluency. You have to experience them as a native speaker says them, repeat them as a native speaker would, and through mass amount of practice come to an innate understanding of the inner workings of a language's morphology. Most native speakers can't explain their own grammar. It just happens.

How to Use GMS and GSR

The best way to use GMS is to find a certain time of day that works best for you where you can concentrate. It doesn't have to be a lot of time, maybe just 30 minutes at most is fine. If you have more time, even better. Then schedule that time to be your study time every day.

Try to tackle anywhere from 20 to 100 sentences per day in the GMS. Do what you're comfortable with.

Review the first 50 sentences in the book to get an idea of what will be said. Then listen to the A files. If you can, try to write all the sentences down from the files as dictation without looking at the text. This will force you to differentiate all the sounds of the language. If you don't like using the A files, you can switch to the C files which only have the target language.

After dictation, check your work for any mistakes. These mistakes should tell you a lot that you will improve on the next day.

Go through the files once again, repeating all the sentences. Then record yourself saying all the sentences. Ideally, you should record these sentences four to five days in a row in order to become very familiar with them.

All of the activities above may take more than one day or one setting, so go at the pace that feels comfortable for you.

If this schedule is too difficult to adhere to, or you find that dictation and recording is too much, then take a more relaxed approach with the GSR files. The GSR files in most cases are shorter than twenty minutes, some go over due to the length of the sentences. But this is the perfect attention span that most people have anyway. By the end of the GSR files you should feel pretty tired, especially if you're trying to repeat everything.

The GSR files are numbered from Day 1 to Day 100. Just do one every day, as all the five days of review sentences are built in. It's that simple! Good luck.

Sentence Mining

Sentence mining can be a fun activity where you find sentences that you like or feel useful in the language you're learning. We suggest keeping your list of sentences in a spreadsheet that you can re-order how you wish.

It's always a good idea to keep a list of all the sentences you're learning or mastering. They not only encompass a lot of vocabulary and their actual usage, or "collocations", but they give you a framework for speaking the language. It's also fun to keep track of your progress and see the number of sentences increasing.

Based on many tests we've conducted, we've found that students can reach a good level of fluency with only a small number of sentences. For example, with just 3000 sentences, each trained 10 times over a period of 5 days, for a total of 30,000 sentences (repetitions), can make a difference between a completely mute person who is shy and unsure how to speak and a talkative person who wants to talk about everything. More importantly, the reps empower you to become a stronger speaker.

The sentences we have included in our Glossika courses have been carefully selected to give you a wide range of expression. The sentences in our fluency modules target the kinds of conversations that you have discussing day-to-day activities, the bulk of what makes up our real-life conversations with friends and family. For some people these sentences may feel really boring, but these sentences are carefully selected to represent an array of discussing events that occur in the past, the present and the future, and whether those actions are continuous or not, even in languages where such grammar is not explicitly marked—especially in these languages as you need to know how to convey your thoughts. The sentences are transparent enough that they give you the tools to go and create dozens of more sentences based on the models we give you.

As you work your way through our Fluency Series the sentences will cover all aspects of grammar without actually teaching you grammar. You'll find most of the patterns used in all the tenses and aspects, passive and active (or ergative as is the case in some languages we're developing), indirect speech, and finally describing events as if to a policeman. The sentences also present some transformational patterns you can look out for. Sometimes we have more than one way to say something in our own language, but maybe only one in a foreign language. And the opposite is true where we may only have one way to say something whereas a foreign language may have many.

Transformation Drills

A transformation is restating the same sentence with the same meaning, but using different words or phrasing to accomplish this. A transformation is essentially a translation, but inside the same language. A real example from Glossika's business module is:

- Could someone help me with my bags?
- Could I get a hand with these bags?

You may not necessarily say "hand" in a foreign language and that's why direct translation word-for-word can be dangerous. As you can see from these two sentences, they're translations of each other, but they express the same meaning.

To express yourself well in a foreign language, practice the art of restating everything you say in your mother language. Find more ways to say the same thing.

There are in fact two kinds of transformation drills we can do. One is transformation in our mother language and the other is transformation into our target language, known as translation.

By transforming a sentence in your own language, you'll get better at transforming it into another language and eventually being able to formulate your ideas and thoughts in that language. It's a process and it won't happen over night. Cultivate your ability day by day.

Build a bridge to your new language through translation. The better you get, the less you rely on the bridge until one day, you won't need it at all.

Translation should never be word for word or literal. You should always aim to achieve the exact same feeling in the foreign language. The only way to achieve this is by someone who can create the sentences for you who already knows both languages to such fluency that he knows the feeling created is exactly the same.

In fact, you'll encounter many instances in our GMS publications where sentences don't seem to match up. The two languages are expressed completely differently, and it seems it's wrong. Believe us, we've not only gone over and tested each sentence in real life situations, we've even refined the translations several times to the point that this is really how we speak in this given situation.

Supplementary Substitution Drills

Substitution drills are more or less the opposite of transformation drills. Instead of restating the same thing in a different way, you're saying a different thing using the exact same way. So using the example from above we can create this substitution drill:

- Could someone help me with my bags?
- Could someone help me with making dinner?

In this case, we have replaced the noun with a gerund phrase. The sentence has a different meaning but it's using the same structure. This drill also allows the learner to recognize a pattern how to use a verb behind a preposition, especially after being exposed to several instances of this type.

We can also combine transformation and substitution drills:

- Could someone help me with my bags?
- Could someone give me a hand with making dinner?

So it is encouraged that as you get more and more experience working through the Glossika materials, that you not only write out and record more and more of your own conversations, but also do more transformation and substitution drills on top of the sentences we have included in the book.

Memory, The Brain, and Language Acquisition

by Michael Campbell

We encounter a lot of new information every day that may or may not need to be memorized. In fact, we're doing it all the time when we make new friends, remembering faces and other information related to our friends.

After some experience with language learning you'll soon discover that languages are just like a social landscape. Except instead of interconnected friends we have interconnected words. In fact, looking at languages in this way makes it a lot more fun as you get familiar with all the data.

Since languages are natural and all humans are able to use them naturally, it only makes sense to learn languages in a natural way. In fact studies have found, and many students having achieved fluency will attest to, the fact that words are much easier to recognize in their written form if we already know them in the spoken form. Remember that you already own the words you use to speak with. The written form is just a record and it's much easier to transfer what you know into written form than trying to memorize something that is only written.

Trying to learn a language from the writing alone can be a real daunting task. Learning to read a language you already speak is not hard at all. So don't beat yourself up trying to learn how to read a complicated script like Chinese if you have no idea how to speak the language yet. It's not as simple as one word = one character. And the same holds true with English as sometimes many words make up one idea, like "get over it".

What is the relationship between memory and sleep? Our brain acquires experiences throughout the day and records them as memories. If these memories are too common, such as eating lunch, they get lost among all the others and we find it difficult to remember one specific memory from the others. More importantly such memories leave no impact or impression on us. However, a major event like a birth or an accident obviously leaves a bigger impact. We attach importance to those events.

Since our brain is constantly recording our daily life, it collects a lot of useless information. Since this information is both mundane and unimportant to us, our brain has a built-in mechanism to deal with it. In other words, our brains dump the garbage every day. Technically speaking our memories are connections between our nerve cells and these connections lose strength if they are not recalled or used again.

During our sleep cycles our brain is reviewing all the events of the day. If you do not recall those events the following day, the memory weakens. After three sleep cycles, consider a memory gone if you haven't recalled it. Some memories can be retained longer because you may have anchored it better the first time you encountered it. An anchor is connecting your memory with one of your senses or another pre-existing memory. During your language learning process, this won't happen until later in your progress. So what can you do in the beginning?

A lot of memory experts claim that making outrageous stories about certain things they're learning help create that anchor where otherwise none would exist. Some memory experts picture a house in their mind that they're very familiar with and walk around that house in a specific pre-arranged order. Then all the objects they're memorizing are placed in that house in specific locations. In order to recall them, they just walk around the house.

I personally have had no luck making outrageous stories to memorize things. I've found the house method very effective but it's different than the particular way I use it. This method is a form of "memory map", or spatial memory, and for me personally I prefer using real world maps. This probably originates from my better than average ability to remember maps, so if you can, then use it! It's not for everybody though. It really works great for learning multiple languages.

What do languages and maps have in common? Everything can be put on a map, and languages naturally are spoken in locations and spread around and change over time. These changes in pronunciations of words creates a word history, or etymology. And by understanding how pronunciations change over time and where populations migrated, it's quite easy to remember a large number of data with just a memory map. This is how I anchor new languages I'm learning. I have a much bigger challenge when I try a new language family. So I look for even deeper and longer etymologies that are shared between language families, anything to help me establish a link to some core vocabulary. Some words like "I" (think Old English "ic") and "me/mine" are essentially the same roots all over the world from Icelandic (Indo-European) to Finnish (Uralic) to Japanese (Altaic?) to Samoan (Austronesian).

I don't confuse languages because in my mind every language sounds unique and has its own accent and mannerisms. I can also use my memory map to position myself in the location where the language is spoken and imagine myself surrounded by the people of that country. This helps me adapt to their expressions and mannerisms, but more importantly, eliminates interference from other languages. And when I mentally set myself up in this way, the chance of confusing a word from another language simply doesn't happen.

When I've actually used a specific way of speaking and I've done it several days in a row, I know that the connections in my head are now strengthening and taking root. Not using them three days in a row creates a complete loss, however actively using them (not passively listening) three days in a row creates a memory that stays for a lifetime. Then you no longer need the anchors and the memory is just a part of you.

You'll have noticed that the Glossika training method gives a translation for every sentence, and in fact we use translation as one of the major anchors for you. In this way 1) the translation acts as an anchor, 2) you have intelligible input, 3) you easily start to recognize patterns. Pattern recognition is the single most important skill you need for learning a foreign language.

A lot of people think that translation should be avoided at all costs when learning a foreign language. However, based on thousands of tests I've given my students over a ten-year period, I've found that just operating in the foreign language itself creates a false sense of understanding and you have a much higher chance of hurting yourself in the long run by creating false realities.

I set up a specific test. I asked my students to translate back into their mother tongue (Chinese) what they heard me saying. These were students who could already hold conversations in English. I found the results rather shocking. Sentences with certain word combinations or phrases really caused a lot of misunderstanding, like "might as well" or "can't do it until", resulted in a lot of guesswork and rather incorrect answers.

If you assume you can think and operate in a foreign language without being able to translate what's being said, you're fooling yourself into false comprehension. Train yourself to translate everything into your foreign language. This again is an anchor that you can eventually abandon when you become very comfortable with the new language.

Finally, our brain really is a sponge. But you have to create the structure of the sponge. Memorizing vocabulary in a language that you don't know is like adding water to a sponge that has no structure: it all flows out.

In order to create a foreign language structure, or "sponge", you need to create sentences that are natural and innate. You start with sentence structures with basic, common vocabulary that's easy enough to master and start building from there. With less than 100 words, you can build thousands of sentences to fluency, slowly one by one adding more and more vocabulary. Soon, you're speaking with natural fluency and you have a working vocabulary of several thousand words.

If you ever learn new vocabulary in isolation, you have to start using it immediately in meaningful sentences. Hopefully sentences you want to use. If you can't make a sentence with it, then the vocabulary is useless.

Vocabulary shouldn't be memorized haphazardly because vocabulary itself is variable. The words we use in our language are only a tool for conveying a larger message, and every language uses different words to convey the same message. Look for the message, pay attention to the specific words used, then learn those words. Memorizing words from a wordlist will not help you with this task.

Recently a friend showed me his wordlist for learning Chinese, using a kind of spaced repetition flashcard program where he could download a "deck". I thought it was a great idea until I saw the words he was trying to learn. I tried explaining that learning these characters out of context do not have the meanings on his cards and they will mislead him into a false understanding, especially individual characters. This would only work if they were a review from a text he had read, where all the vocabulary appeared in real sentences and a story to tell, but they weren't. From a long-term point of view, I could see that it would hurt him and require twice as much time to re-learn everything. From the short-term point of view, there was definitely a feeling of progress and mastery and he was happy with that and I dropped the issue.

French Background and Pronunciation

- **Classification:** Indo-European Language Family - Romance Branch
- **Writing:** Latin

- **Consonants:**

  /p b f v m t d s z l n ʃ ʒ j ɲ ɥ k g ʁ w/ Unvoiced stops (p, t, k) are not aspirated /pᵊ tᵊ kᵊ/ different from English.

- **Vowels:**

  /i y u e ø ə o ɛ œ ɔ ɛ̃ ɔ̃ ɑ̃ a ɑ/

- **IPA:** Phonetic transcription showing liaison

- **Intonation:** Mostly word-final and even phrase-final
- **Word Order:** Subject - Verb - Object
- **Adjective Order:** Noun - Adjective
- **Possessive Order:** Genitive - Noun
- **Adposition Order:** Preposition - Noun
- **Dependent Clause:** Dependent - Noun, Noun - Relative Clause
- **Verbs:** Tense (present, past, future), Aspect (perfect, imperfect), Mood (indicative, subjunctive)
- **Nouns:** 2 genders, definite/indefinite
- **Pronouns:** 1st/2nd/3rd, masc/feminine/neuter, singular/plural, reflexive, 6 conjugations

Classification

French is closely related to the other Romance languages (languages of the Romans) descended from Latin. Historically all of these languages are generalisations of a dialect continuum from Italy up to France and then down to the Iberian peninsula where Catalan, Spanish and Portuguese are spoken. Today we like to give things labels such as "language" or "dialect", but the difference between them can cause disputes. Historically, there were only dialects. It wasn't until nation states sprung up and communication required a standard that languages were standardized, usually based on the "dialect" of the capital city. In some countries like Italy, when it was unified in the 19th century a national language was created with bits and pieces from various dialects spoken around the new "country". These national, standardized "languages" become a nation's identity to the rest of the world.

So as we can identify a central position among a dialectal region, perhaps a place of commerce or larger city, the speech of areas between these places of commerce become dialectal grey areas where the continuum blends slowly into the next. So from the northern region of Italy where people speak a national Italian language and a local dialect, they can just as easily switch between their local dialect and the neighboring French language, simply because their dialect is at the halfway point between the two national languages. Likewise those in southern France may also be able to communicate with Italians in the border areas. In southern France one finds the language of the "Ocs" because they say "òc" instead of "oui" for the word "yes". This language, Occitan (or Provençal) has its own dialectal regions, but it is gradually blends into the "Catalan" of Spain. Our Glossika course for "Catalan" is based on the speech of Barcelona, but you could still use it to communicate in or acquire "Occitan" in southern France. It should be seen as an intermediary language between French, Spanish and Italian.

One might wonder how dialects came about in the first place. Languages evolve naturally, and like biological evolution, the traits that are adopted by the masses are those that continue to live on from one generation to the next. No one individual can take control over the future course of a language or how it evolves. But then you may wonder, how can a national language be created and how can it be adopted by everyone in the country? The matter is not as simple as you may think. What happens in most cases (or we could say, in most countries) is a dual register. If you are from England, then you will definitely be aware of the regional dialects and how words and sometimes how grammar differs from area to area. The English language also differs between different classes of people, from the poor to the rich, historically one's speech defines a man's social status.

The Académie française, restored in its modern form by Napoleon in 1803, polices the French language as a national standard. So on the one hand we can say that no individual person or "academy" can control a language's evolution, on the other hand it is precisely for this reason that the Académie has been established, so that a standard of speech can be maintained among all the dialects within France. To this day, as in most countries, a dichotomy remains: the local dialects in all their flavours, and the national standard. It is quite possible that as a student of the language you will eventually learn how to recognize and switch between them yourself, depending on the circumstances and your audience.

Due to the dichotomy that exists in most languages (the real world spoken dialect vs. the national standard), most textbooks only teach the national standard and there are peculiarities with the colloquial language that is seldom taught. It is our goal here at Glossika to present you with the real spoken language, not in defiance of the national standard, but to allow you as the student to get as close as humanly possible to communicating comfortably in social settings in your host country. This means that in a language like French which has a lot of tricky pronunciation with liaison, that what you will learn from this course is the relaxed and comfortable liaisons rather than the official ones. This will make it possible to meet people and let them feel comfortable with your style of speech from the very beginning. Oftentimes speaking exactly like a textbook or text-to-speech algorithm will not benefit you socially as much as you would like it to.

Thus the language presented in the Glossika recordings are based on the national standard, but the liaisons are spoken in a relaxed way. We do not need to change the spelling or the text in any way to show this (unlike our Finnish, Armenian and Persian courses which require parallel texts due to the dichotomy), however our phonetic transcription is written in such a way that it matches the surface pronunciation that you will encounter in the sound files.

Grammar

This fluency series of books does not go into grammatical detail. This is why we recommend to use this course as a supplement to other studies, but if you are using it alone, then you can get a lot of the grammatical explanation online from Wikipedia and videos that teachers have shared. Since French is a widely taught language, we will not attempt to replicate any grammatical explanations in this course. The Glossika Fluency series really focus on speaking the language in real life, so all of your effort in this course should be spent on accent and pronunciation improvement, both in speaking and listening.

Since the course is written with syntax structure in mind, it should follow a natural sequence of ever more complex sentences, of which you will find many deliberate iterations therein in order to allow to acquire a true natural and fluent grasp of the language. The goal of this definition of fluency is not a huge vocabulary, but rather complete freedom over your ability to manipulate sentences.

The most important feature of this course is our list of words and all their variable pronunciations that occur throughout the course which we will describe below in more detail.

Due to differences between your language and French, we advise you never to get stuck analyzing just one sentence. Sometimes word orders are different. Oftentimes there is not enough data in one sentence to deduce what is happening. To take this method to heart, start of by going through the whole book listening to all 1000 sentences and take some occasional notes when you notice patterns. By learning how to notice these patterns, you are building the skills you need for natural language acquisition. Don't try to memorize any single sentence or any grammatical rules. Get a feel for how the sentences flow off the tongue.

The native speaker will speak long strings of syllables in such rapid succession that you'll find it impossible to follow or imitate in the beginning. This is due to the aforementioned problem: too small of a data set to extract or deduce what you need to learn. To learn effectively, or whenever you get stuck, just sit back with your book and relax, play through all 1000 sentences in a single setting and let the repetitive parts of the phrases fill your ears and your brain. Soon you'll be on the right track to mimicking these phrases just as a child does. A child will always have a rough approximation of speech before the age of five, but has no problem in saying complete sentences. So always focus first on fluency and continue to work hard on perfecting your pronunciation, intonation, and accent.

As a foreigner, it may take you many years to master the language. We've given you about six to twelve months of training here depending on your personal schedule. Everything included here is just the basic of basics, so you really need to get to the point where all of these sentences become quite easy to manipulate and produce, and then you can spend the next five to ten years conversing in French and learning how to say more and more, learning directly inside the language without the need for translating. We've given you the tools to get to that point.

Structure

French stress evolved out of Latin stress, so the stress patterns are almost identical to those found in Italian, Catalan, Spanish and Portuguese. But since a lot of phonological degradation has occurred in French over the centuries, the penultimate stress you find in Italian and Spanish has become final stress in both French and Catalan (Occitan). French has been moving more and more to a non-stress pattern as words get shorter and shorter getting strung together in rapid succession, and in most cases you'll find that stress on individual words has disappeared and has moved to the end of the phrase. This is usually the case in fluent speech. This has also given rise to innovations in the language, for example "pas" placed after the negated verb, because the negative participle can almost get completely lost in speech due to nasalization and shortening of words. And so in almost every instance of "pas", you'll find it with a strong stress as to make sure the phrase is understood as being negative.

Unlike Italian or Spanish, the diacritics above letters in French do not indicate stress patterns at all. These are used simply to indicate different pronunciations. For example, the letter {e} can very easily disappear or be swallowed by neighboring consonants (in which case we write as a tiny superscript schwa [°] as a possible phonetic realization). If the letter {e} is still to be pronounced, it depends on its position (is it followed by {-s} or {-t} or {-z} at the end of a word?) or it would be written with an acute accent {é}. In this case it should sound like its IPA equivalent /e/. The other two letters {è, ê} are both pronounced like the English short vowel /ɛ/. The letter {ê} in most cases gave rise from a disappearing {-s} as can be observed in "même" (Spanish: mismo) and "forêt" (English: forest) and other evolutions of the language. Likewise the letter {é} can also represent the disappearing {-s} at the beginning of words which can be observed in "étude" (Spanish: estudio, English: study).

Names

The Glossika Fluency series is a global production with over a hundred languages in development, so we include names from all the major languages and cultures around the world. Many of these are foreign to French speakers, and probably including yourself. However, it is of particular interest to us how languages deal with foreign names, both in localizing and dealing with them grammatically. In this edition we have not attempted to write the pronunciation of names, but left the pronunciation up to the native speaker. However, note how word endings are attached to names, because as a foreigner speaking French, you will undoubtedly have to use foreign names. Also use these names to your advantage, as an anchor in each sentence to figure out how all the other parts of speech interact with the name.

The pronunciation guide used in this book (please read the following section for details) does not account for foreign words or borrowings and so we simply do not transcribe the pronunciations in this case.

IPA

Almost all language teaching books over the last century have resorted to awkward explanations of pronunciation. You may have seen lots of strange pronunciation guides over the years in all kinds of publications. The problem with these kinds of publications is many-fold. Many times the pronunciation being taught is very specific to American pronunciation in particular, which means even if you're not American, you'll end up pronouncing the language you're learning like an American. I've seen similar devices used in British publications, but many times when I see a book explain: "pronounce it like the vowel in 'hear'" I have no idea which version of

English they're referring to. The British books often make references to Scottish speakers, which is not really common knowledge for Americans. So I think it is important to consider where your readers are coming from without making assumptions.

The second problem is why would anybody want to pronounce the language they're learning like an American? Isn't the point to learn pronunciation as closely as we can to the way native speakers speak? In any case, it pays off well to work hard at eliminating a trace of one's foreign accent when speaking other languages. It also puts your listeners at ease as they won't have to strain so hard to understand what you're saying. Here we will avoid criticizing all the problems related to the transcription of other pronunciation guides and why they may be misleading, and focus our attention instead to amazing solutions.

Over the last century our knowledge of phonetics has improved greatly. All of this knowledge seems to have been known by the elite few professors and students of Linguistics departments scattered around the globe. But with the internet comes the explosion of information that is now accessible to everybody. Not only that, but language learners, even average language learners, are a lot smarter about the process of going about learning other languages than people were just a mere twenty or thirty years ago. It is now possible for teenagers to achieve fluency in any number of languages they want from the comfort of their own home just by using the resources available on the internet. I personally attempted to do so when I was a teenager without the internet, and trying to make sense of languages with very little data or explanation was quite frustrating.

As well-informed language learners of the twenty-first century, we now have access to all the tools that make languages much easier to learn. If you can read other languages as well, there are literally thousands of blogs, discussion groups, communities and places to go on the internet to learn everything you want to know about language learning. There is still a lot of misinformation getting passed around, but the community is maturing. The days of using such hackneyed pronunciation guides are hopefully over.

All the secrets that linguists have had are now available to the general public. Linguists have been using the International Phonetic Alphabet (IPA) as a standard for recording languages, where every letter is given one and only one sound, what is called a point of articulation. This enables linguists to talk about linguistic phenomena in a scientific and precise way. Since the point of articulation can be slightly different from language to language, a single letter like /t/ does not have a very specific point, but just a general area that we can call "alveolar" the location known as the alveolar ridge behind the teeth. IPA has extra diacritics available to indicate where the /t/ is to be pronounced. In a lot of cases, this information is not necessary for talking about the language in broad terms, especially topics unrelated to pronunciation, so as long as the language has no other kind of /t/ in that same area, there's no need to indicate the precise location: this is known as phonemic.

English is a good example. For example, we don't think about it much that {t} is pronounced differently in "take", "wanted", "letter", "stuff" and "important". If you're North American, the {t} in each of these words is actually pronounced differently: aspirated, as a nasal, as a flap, unaspirated, as a glottal stop. Maybe you never even realized it. But to a foreign learner of English, hearing all these different sounds can get very confusing especially when everybody says "it's a T!" but in reality they're saying different things. It's not that Americans don't hear the different sounds, it's just that they label all of the sounds as {t} which leads them to believe that what they're actually hearing are the same. But it more difficult for the foreigners to learn when a {t} is pronounced as a glottal stop or as a flap, etc. The task for the language learner is often underestimated by teachers and native speakers.

Many letters in English have these variations which are called "allophones" and we can record them as separate letters in IPA or with diacritical marks. In order to indicate that this pronunciation is "precise" I should use square brackets: [tʰ, t̚, ɾ, ʔ]. So we can say that although English has one phonemic /t/, in reality there are many allophones. Actually every language has allophones! So what we learn as spelling, or in a book, usually is just the general phonemic guide, and it differs quite a bit from the way people actually speak with allophones. When I'm learning a foreign language I always ask what the allophones are because it helps me speak that language much clearer and much more like a native.

Why does a language learner need a "precise" pronunciation guide?

Let's take the English learner again. If that person is told to always pronounce {t} exactly the same way, then his speech will actually become very emphatic, unnatural sounding and forced. To native speakers this learner will always have a strong foreign accent, have choppy pronunciation and be difficult to understand. We should always set our goals high enough even if we can't attain them perfectly, but at least we're pushing ourselves to achieve more than we would have otherwise. So if you have an accurate transcription of native speakers which indicates all the variations that they use, you will have access to a wealth of information that no other language learner had access to before. Not only that but you have the tools available for perfecting your pronunciation.

There is no better solution than IPA itself, the secret code of the linguists. Now the IPA is available in Wikipedia with links for each letter to separate pages with recordings and a list of languages that use those sounds.

From the beginning you must take note that French has absolutely no aspirated sounds, so that the English {p, t, k} are completely different from French {p, t, k}. To summarize:

English {p, t, k} = lots of aspiration (puff of air) French {p, t, k} = no aspiration whatsoever. To the untrained English ear, they may actually sound like {b, d, g}, which means you'll need more exposure and practice.

French Pronunciation

The IPA transcription in this book is based on a computer program written by the Glossika staff which produces pronunciation in two steps which is required for all languages: 1) phonemic, 2) phonetic. The computer program is based on the official spelling of the language alone rather than pronunciation guides. Some languages require additional steps of adding stress and tone in order to get the correct phonetic output, as in the case for French "appele" and "appeler", otherwise the unstressed {e} in the second example would get deleted.

Liaison is a big issue that any student of French is acutely aware of. Our transcription works like this:

1. If the ending of a word is not pronounced, the phonemes get deleted.
2. If the ending of a word carries over to the next word, the phoneme moves to the next word and *starts* it.
3. If a word contains the sometimes pronounced schwa, we write it as [°] or which some speakers do not pronounce. This results in consonant "clusters", but consonant clusters occur in two different ways among world languages:

A) Languages with consonant clusters that fuse together: English, Russian, German, etc. B) Languages with consonant clusters where every consonant is spoken individually with an epenthetic [°]: French, Georgian, Atayal, etc.

In other words, consonant clusters in English and French are produced differently. Where you come across [db] in "debout" does not sound like the [db] in English "bad boy", but rather spoken slightly separately as [d°b]. An English speaker would consider "bad° boy" with an epenthetic [°] an incorrect pronunciation, whereas this is not the case in French.

Last two pieces of advice: Please consult the IPA transcription whenever in doubt.

Don't forget that if you ever get frustrated, just go back through all 1000 sentences and relax while you listen. No need to force yourself to remember or repeat during this. This is just to help clear your mind of a few problematic sentences. Chances are, if you keep moving through all the sentences, those troublesome sentences will no longer be troublesome when you loop back around again.

Vocabulary Index

1. The vocabulary index does not include foreign names and places, or words without an IPA transcription.
2. The index lists every variation of every French word found in this book. However, for common words, we do not list every single sentence in which they occur in order to save space. The first few sentences that we do list should be enough of a resource for you to check that special occurrence or pronunciation pattern.
3. Words that are combined in transcription in the text are separated in the index for individual lookup.
4. All words that have a change in liaison can be looked up in the index by observing the IPA transcription. Do you want to know when "tous" is pronounced [tu] or [tus]? Do you want to know when "allé" is pronounced [ale] or [zale] or [tale] because of the preceding liaison? Do you want to know how many different conjugations appear in our text? All of these are listed as separate entries in the index for your convenience.

We sincerely hope that our unique way of presenting the language will be useful for both students and teachers alike and will remain as a useful reference and tool for years to come.

Vocabulary: French

Prepositions

about	sur
above	au-dessus
according to	selon
across	à travers
after	après
against	contre
among	entre
around	autour de
as	comme
as far as	autant que
as well as	aussi bien que
at	à
because of	en raison de
before	avant
behind	derrière
below	en dessous
beneath	sous
beside	à côté de
between	entre
beyond	au-delà
but	mais
by	par
close to	près de
despite	malgré

down	vers le bas
due to	à cause de
during	au cours de
except	sauf
except for	à l'exception de
far from	loin d'être
for	pour
from	à partir de
in	dans
in addition to	en plus de
in front of	en face de
in spite of	en dépit de
inside	à l'intérieur
inside of	l'intérieur de
instead of	au lieu de
into	dans
near	près de
near to	près de
next	prochain
next to	à côté de
of	de
on	sur
on behalf of	au nom de
on top of	au sommet de
opposite	opposé
out	à
outside	à l'extérieur
outside of	en dehors des
over	sur

per	par
plus	plus
prior to	avant
round	tour
since	depuis
than	que
through	par
till	jusqu'à
to	à
toward	vers
under	sous
unlike	contrairement à
until	jusqu'à ce que
up	jusqu'à
via	via
with	avec
within	dans
without	sans

Adjectives

a few	quelques
bad	mauvais
big	grand
bitter	amer
clean	propre
correct	correct
dark	sombre
deep	profond

difficult	difficile
dirty	sale
dry	sec
easy	facile
empty	vide
expensive	cher
fast	rapide
few	peu
foreign	étranger
fresh	frais
full	plein
good	bon
hard	dur
heavy	lourd
inexpensive	peu coûteux
light	léger
little	peu
local	local
long	long
many	beaucoup
much	beaucoup
narrow	étroit
new	nouveau
noisy	bruyant
old	vieux
part	partie
powerful	puissant
quiet	calme
short person	salé

small	court
salty	lent
slow	petit
soft	doux
some	certains
sour	aigre
spicy	épicé
sweet	doux
tall	haut
thick	épais
thin	mince
very	très
weak	faible
wet	humide
whole	ensemble
wide	large
wrong	faux
young	jeune

Adverbs

absolutely	absolument
ago	il y a
almost	presque
alone	seul
already	déjà
always	toujours
anywhere	n'importe où
away	loin

barely	à peine
carefully	soigneusement
everywhere	partout
fast	rapide
frequently	fréquemment
hard	dur
hardly	à peine
here	ici
home	maison
immediately	immédiatement
last night	dernière nuit
lately	récemment
later	plus tard
mostly	surtout
never	jamais
next week	semaine prochaine
now	maintenant
nowhere	nulle part
occasionally	de temps en temps
out	dehors
over there	là-bas
pretty	joli
quickly	rapidement
quite	tout à fait, assez
rarely	rarement
really	vraiment
recently	récemment
right now	pour le moment, en ce moment
seldom	rarement

slowly	lentement
sometimes	parfois
soon	bientôt
still	encore
then	puis
there	là
this morning	ce matin
today	aujourd'hui
together	ensemble
tomorrow	demain
tonight	ce soir
usually	habituellement
very	très
well	bien
yesterday	hier, la vielle
yet	encore

Glossika Mass Sentences

GMS #1 - 100

1

EN The weather's nice today.

FR Il fait beau aujourd'hui.
IPA [il fɛ bo oʒuʁdɥi ||]

2

EN I'm not rich.

FR Je ne suis pas riche.
IPA [ʒø nø sɥi pa ʁiʃ ||]

3

EN This bag's heavy.

FR Ce sac est lourd.
IPA [sø sak e luʁ ||]

4

EN These bags are heavy.

FR Ces sacs sont lourds.
IPA [se sak sɔ̃ luʁ ||]

5

EN Look, there's my friend.

FR Regarde, voilà mon ami.
IPA [ʁ°gaʁd | vwala mɔ̃ n̩ami ||]

6

EN My brother and I are good tennis players.

FR Mon frère et moi sommes de bons joueurs de tennis.
IPA [mɔ̃ fʁɛʁ e mwa sɔm də bɔ̃ ʒwœʁ də tenis ||]

7

EN His mother's at home. He's at school.

FR Sa mère est à la maison. Il est à l'école.
IPA [sa mɛʁ e a la mɛzɔ̃ || i l̩e a l̩ekɔl ||]

8

EN Her children are at school.

FR Ses enfants sont à l'école.
IPA [se z̩ɑ̃fɑ̃ sɔ̃ a l̩ekɔl ||]

9

EN I'm a taxi driver.

FR Je suis chauffeur de taxi.
IPA [ʒø sɥi ʃofœʁ də taksi ||]

10

EN My sister's a nurse.

FR Ma sœur est infirmière.
IPA [ma sœʁ e t‿ɛ̃fiʁmjeʁ ‖]

11

EN He's sick. He's in bed.

FR Il est malade. Il est au lit.
IPA [i l‿e malad ‖ i l‿e o li ‖]

12

EN I'm not hungry, but I'm thirsty.

FR Je n'ai pas faim, mais j'ai soif.
IPA [ʒø n‿ɛ pa fɛ̃ | mɛ ʒ‿ɛ swaf ‖]

13

EN He's a very old man. He's ninety-eight (98) years old.

FR Il est un très vieil homme. Il a quatre-vingt-dix-huit ans.
IPA [i l‿e t‿œ̃ tʁɛ vjej l‿ɔm ‖ i l‿a katʁ°vɛ̃dizɥi t‿ɑ̃ ‖]

14

EN These chairs aren't beautiful, but they're comfortable.

FR Ces chaises ne sont pas très belles, mais elles sont confortables.
IPA [se ʃɛz nø sɔ̃ pa tʁɛ bɛl | mɛ ɛl sɔ̃ kɔ̃fɔʁtabl ‖]

15

EN The weather's warm and sunny today.

FR Il fait chaud et ensoleillé aujourd'hui.
IPA [il fɛ ʃo e ɑ̃soleje oʒuʁdɥi ‖]

16

EN You're late. — No, I'm not! I'm early.

FR Tu es en retard. — Non, je ne le suis pas! Je suis en avance.
IPA [ty ɛ ɑ̃ ʁ°taʁ ‖ — nɔ̃ | ʒø nø lø sɥi pa ‖ ʒø sɥi z‿ɑ̃ n‿avɑ̃s ‖]

17

EN She isn't home. She's at work.

FR Elle n'est pas à la maison. Elle est au travail.
IPA [ɛl n‿e pa a la mɛzɔ̃ ‖ ɛ l‿e o tʁavaj ‖]

18

EN Here's your coat.

FR Voici ton manteau.
IPA [vwasi tɔ̃ mɑ̃to ‖]

19

EN What's your name?

FR Comment t'appelles-tu?
IPA [komɑ̃ t‿apɛl ty ‖]

20

EN My name's Alan.

FR Je m'appelle Alan.
IPA [ʒø m‿apɛl (...) ‖]

21

EN Where are you from?

FR D'où viens-tu?
IPA [d‿u vjɛ̃ ty ‖]

22

EN I'm from New York.

FR Je viens de New York.
IPA [ʒø vjɛ̃ dø nuw jɔʁk ‖]

23

EN How old are you?

FR Quel âge as-tu?
IPA [kɛ l‿aʒ a ty ‖]

24

EN I'm twenty (20) years old.

FR J'ai vingt ans.
IPA [ʒ‿ɛ vɛ̃ t‿ɑ̃ ‖]

25

EN What's your job?

FR Quel est ton métier?
IPA [kɛ lˑe tɔ̃ metje ||]

26

EN I'm a teacher.

FR Je suis enseignant (♀enseignante).
IPA [ʒø sɥi ãsɛɲã (♀ãsɛɲãt) ||]

27

EN What's your favorite color?

FR Quelle est ta couleur préférée?
IPA [kɛ lˑe ta kulœʁ pʁefeʁe ||]

28

EN My favorite color is blue.

FR Ma couleur préférée est le bleu.
IPA [ma kulœʁ pʁefeʁe e lø blø ||]

29

EN What are you interested in?

FR À quoi t'intéresses-tu? > Quels sont tes intérêts?
IPA [a kwa t‿ɛ̃teʁɛs ty || > kɛl sɔ̃ te z‿ɛ̃teʁɛ ||]

30

EN I'm interested in music.

FR Je m'intéresse à la musique.
IPA [ʒø m‿ɛ̃teʁɛs a la myzik ‖]

31

EN It's hot today.

FR Il fait chaud aujourd'hui.
IPA [il fɛ ʃo oʒuʁdɥi ‖]

32

EN It isn't hot today.

FR Il ne fait pas chaud aujourd'hui.
IPA [il nø fɛ pa ʃo oʒuʁdɥi ‖]

33

EN It's windy today.

FR C'est venteux aujourd'hui.
IPA [sɛ vɑ̃tø oʒuʁdɥi ‖]

34

EN It isn't windy today.

FR Ce n'est pas venteux aujourd'hui.
IPA [sø n‿e pa vɑ̃tø oʒuʁdɥi ‖]

35

EN My hands are cold.

FR Mes mains sont froides.
IPA [me mɛ̃ sɔ̃ fʁwad ‖]

36

EN Brazil is a very big country.

FR Le Brésil est un très grand pays.
IPA [lø bʁezil e t‿ɛ̃ tʁɛ gʁɑ̃ pei ‖]

37

EN Diamonds are not cheap.

FR Les diamants ne sont pas bon marché.
IPA [le djamɑ̃ nø sɔ̃ pa bɔ̃ maʁʃe ‖]

38

EN Toronto isn't in the United States.

FR Toronto n'est pas aux États-Unis.
IPA [(...) n‿e pa z‿o z‿etazuni ‖]

39

EN I'm tired.

FR Je suis fatigué (♀ fatiguée).
IPA [ʒø sɥi fatige (♀ fatige) ‖]

40

EN I'm not tired.

FR Je ne suis pas fatigué (♀ fatiguée).
IPA [ʒø nø sɥi pa fatige (♀ fatige) ||]

41

EN I'm hungry.

FR J'ai faim.
IPA [ʒ‿ɛ fɛ̃ ||]

42

EN I'm not hungry.

FR Je n'ai pas faim.
IPA [ʒø n‿ɛ pa fɛ̃ ||]

43

EN He's a good swimmer.

FR Il est bon nageur.
IPA [i l‿e bɔ̃ naʒœʁ ||]

44

EN I'm not interested in politics.

FR Je ne m'intéresse pas à la politique.
IPA [ʒø nø m‿ɛ̃teʁɛs pa a la politik ||]

45

EN What's your name?

FR Comment t'appelles-tu?
IPA [kɔmɑ̃ t‿apɛl ty ‖]

46

EN My name's Amanda.

FR Je m'appelle Amanda.
IPA [ʒø m‿apɛl (...) ‖]

47

EN Are you married?

FR Es-tu marié (♀mariée)?
IPA [ɛ ty maʁje (♀maʁje) ‖]

48

EN No, I'm single.

FR Non, je suis célibataire.
IPA [nɔ̃ | ʒø sɥi selibatɛʁ ‖]

49

EN How old are you?

FR Quel âge as-tu?
IPA [kɛ l‿aʒ a ty ‖]

50

EN I'm twenty-five (25).

FR J'ai vingt-cinq ans.
IPA [ʒ‿ɛ vɛ̃tsɛ̃ k‿ɑ̃ ||]

51

EN Are you a student?

FR Es-tu étudiant (♀étudiante)?
IPA [ɛ ty etydjɑ̃ (♀etydjɑ̃t) ||]

52

EN Yes, I am.

FR Oui, je le suis.
IPA [wi | ʒø lø sɥi ||]

53

EN Am I late?

FR Suis-je en retard?
IPA [sɥi ʒø ɑ̃ ʁᵊtaʁ ||]

54

EN No, you're on time.

FR Non, tu es à l'heure.
IPA [nɔ̃ | ty ɛ a l‿œʁ ||]

55

EN Is your mother at home?

FR Ta mère est-elle à la maison?
IPA [ta mɛʁ e t‿ɛl a la mɛzɔ̃ ‖]

56

EN No, she's out.

FR Non, elle est à l'extérieur.
IPA [nɔ̃ | ɛ l‿e a l‿ɛkstɛʁjœʁ ‖]

57

EN Are your parents at home?

FR Tes parents sont-ils à la maison?
IPA [te paʁɑ̃ sɔ̃ t‿il a la mɛzɔ̃ ‖]

58

EN No, they're out.

FR Non, ils sont à l'extérieur.
IPA [nɔ̃ | il sɔ̃ a l‿ɛkstɛʁjœʁ ‖]

59

EN Is it cold in your room?

FR Fait-il froid dans ta chambre?
IPA [fɛ t‿il fʁwa dɑ̃ ta ʃɑ̃bʁ ‖]

60

EN Yes, a little.

FR Oui, un peu.
IPA [wi | œ̃ pø ‖]

61

EN Your shoes are nice. Are they new?

FR Tes chaussures sont jolies. Sont-elles neuves?
IPA [te ʃosyʁ sɔ̃ ʒoli ‖ sɔ̃ t‿ɛl nœv ‖]

62

EN Yes, they are.

FR Oui, elles le sont.
IPA [wi | ɛl lø sɔ̃ ‖]

63

EN Where's your mother? Is she at home?

FR Où est ta mère? Est-elle à la maison?
IPA [u e ta mɛʁ ‖ e t‿ɛl a la mɛzɔ̃ ‖]

64

EN Where are you from?

FR D'où viens-tu?
IPA [d‿u vjɛ̃ ty ‖]

65

EN I'm from Canada.

FR Je viens du Canada.
IPA [ʒø vjɛ̃ dy kanada |||]

66

EN What color is your car?

FR De quelle couleur est ta voiture?
IPA [dø kɛl kulœʁ e ta vwatyʁ |||]

67

EN It's red.

FR Elle est rouge.
IPA [ɛ l̩ e ʁuʒ |||]

68

EN How old is Hassan?

FR Quel âge a Hassan?
IPA [kɛ l̩ aʒ a (...) |||]

69

EN He's twenty-four (24).

FR Il a vingt-quatre ans.
IPA [i l̩ a vɛ̃tkatʁ ɑ̃ |||]

70

EN How are your parents?

FR Comment vont tes parents?
IPA [komã võ te paʁɑ̃ ‖]

71

EN They're doing fine.

FR Ils vont bien.
IPA [il võ bjɛ̃ ‖]

72

EN These postcards are nice. How much are they?

FR Ces cartes postales sont jolies. Combien sont-elles?
IPA [se kaʁt pɔstal sõ ʒoli ‖ kõbjɛ̃ sõ t‿ɛl ‖]

73

EN They're a dollar (USD). They're a pound (GBP).
They're a euro (EUR).

FR Elles sont un euro.
IPA [ɛl sõ t‿œ̃ n‿øʁo ‖]

74

EN This hotel isn't very good. Why is it so expensive?

FR Cet hôtel n'est pas très bon. Pourquoi est-il si cher?
IPA [sɛ t‿otɛl n‿e pa tʁɛ bõ ‖ puʁkwa e t‿il si ʃɛʁ ‖]

75

EN What's your phone number?

FR Quel est ton numéro de téléphone?
IPA [kɛ l̪e tɔ̃ nymeʁo dø telefɔn ‖]

76

EN Who's that man?

FR Qui est cet homme?
IPA [ki e sɛ t̪ɔm ‖]

77

EN He's the boss.

FR C'est le patron.
IPA [sɛ lø patʁɔ̃ ‖]

78

EN Where's your friend?

FR Où est ton amie?
IPA [u e tɔ̃ n̪ami ‖]

79

EN She's in the bathroom.

FR Elle est à la salle de bain.
IPA [ɛ l̪e a la sal dø bɛ̃ ‖]

80

EN How's your father?

FR Comment va ton père?
IPA [komã va tɔ̃ pɛʁ ‖]

81

EN He's doing great.

FR Il va très bien.
IPA [il va tʁɛ bjɛ̃ ‖]

82

EN Are you tired?

FR Es-tu fatigué (♀ fatiguée)?
IPA [ɛ ty fatige (♀ fatige) ‖]

83

EN Yes, I am.

FR Oui, je le suis.
IPA [wi | ʒø lø sɥi ‖]

84

EN Are you hungry?

FR As-tu faim?
IPA [a ty fɛ̃ ‖]

85

EN No, but I'm thirsty.

FR Non, mais j'ai soif.
IPA [nɔ̃ | mɛ ʒ‿ɛ swaf ‖]

86

EN Is your friend Chinese?

FR Ton ami est-il Chinois?
IPA [tɔ̃ n‿ami e t‿il ʃinwa ‖]

87

EN Yes, he is.

FR Oui, il l'est.
IPA [wi | il l‿e ‖]

88

EN Are these your keys?

FR Ce sont tes clés?
IPA [sø sɔ̃ te kle ‖]

89

EN Yes, they are.

FR Oui, ce sont les miennes.
IPA [wi | sø sɔ̃ le mjɛn ‖]

90

EN That's my seat.

FR C'est mon siège.
IPA [sɛ mɔ̃ sjɛʒ ‖]

91

EN No, it isn't.

FR Non, ce ne l'est pas.
IPA [nɔ̃ | sø nø le pa ‖]

92

EN Where's the camera?

FR Où est la caméra?
IPA [u e la kameʁa ‖]

93

EN It's in your bag.

FR Elle est dans ton sac.
IPA [ɛ le dɑ̃ tɔ̃ sak ‖]

94

EN Is your car blue?

FR Ta voiture est-elle bleue?
IPA [ta vwatyʁ e tɛl blø ‖]

95

EN No, it's black.

FR Non, elle est noire.
IPA [nɔ̃ | ɛ l̡e nwaʁ ‖]

96

EN Is Lisa from Toronto?

FR Lisa est-elle de Toronto?
IPA [lisa e t̡ɛl dø (...) ‖]

97

EN No, she's American.

FR Non, elle est Américaine.
IPA [nɔ̃ | ɛ l̡e t̡ameʁiken ‖]

98

EN Am I late?

FR Suis-je en retard?
IPA [sɥi ʒø ɑ̃ ʁᵊtaʁ ‖]

99

EN Yes, you are.

FR Oui, tu l'es.
IPA [wi | ty l̡ɛ ‖]

100

EN Where's Layla from?

FR D'où vient Layla?

IPA [d̪u vjɛ̃ (...) ‖]

GMS #101 - 200

101

EN She's from London.

FR Elle vient de Londres.
IPA [ɛl vjɛ̃ də lɔ̃dʁ° ||]

102

EN What color is your bag?

FR De quelle couleur est ton sac?
IPA [də kɛl kulœʁ e tɔ̃ sak ||]

103

EN It's black.

FR Il est noir.
IPA [i l̩e nwaʁ ||]

104

EN Are you hungry?

FR As-tu faim?
IPA [a ty fɛ̃ ||]

105

EN No, I'm not.

FR Non, je n'ai pas faim.
IPA [nɔ̃ | ʒø n‿ɛ pa fɛ̃ ‖]

106

EN How's John?

FR Comment va John?
IPA [komɑ̃ va (...) ‖]

107

EN He's fine.

FR Il va bien.
IPA [il va bjɛ̃ ‖]

108

EN Who's that woman?

FR Qui est cette femme?
IPA [ki e sɛt fam ‖]

109

EN She's my sister.

FR C'est ma sœur.
IPA [sɛ ma sœʁ ‖]

110

EN Is your mother at home?

FR Ta mère est-elle à la maison?
IPA [ta mɛʁ e t‿ɛl a la mɛzɔ̃ ‖]

111

EN How are your parents?

FR Comment vont tes parents?
IPA [komɑ̃ vɔ̃ te paʁɑ̃ ‖]

112

EN Is your job interesting?

FR Ton travail est-il intéressant?
IPA [tɔ̃ tʁavaj e t‿il ɛ̃teʁɛsɑ̃ ‖]

113

EN Are the stores open today?

FR Les magasins sont-ils ouverts aujourd'hui?
IPA [le magazɛ̃ sɔ̃ t‿il uvɛʁ oʒuʁdɥi ‖]

114

EN Where are you from?

FR D'où viens-tu?
IPA [d‿u vjɛ̃ ty ‖]

115

EN Are you interested in sports?

FR T'intéresses-tu au sport?
IPA [t‿ɛ̃teʁɛs ty o spɔʁ ‖]

116

EN Is the post office near here?

FR Le bureau de poste est-il près d'ici?
IPA [lø byʁo dø pɔst e t‿il pʁɛ d‿isi ‖]

117

EN Are your children at school?

FR Tes enfants sont-ils à l'école?
IPA [te z‿ɑ̃fɑ̃ sɔ̃ t‿il a l‿ekɔl ‖]

118

EN Why are you late?

FR Pourquoi es-tu en retard?
IPA [puʁkwa ɛ ty ɑ̃ ʁᵊtaʁ ‖]

119

EN How are your children?

FR Comment vont tes enfants?
IPA [kɔmɑ̃ vɔ̃ te z‿ɑ̃fɑ̃ ‖]

120

EN They're fine.

FR Ils vont bien.
IPA [il vɔ̃ bjɛ̃ ||]

121

EN Where's the bus stop?

FR Où est l'arrêt de bus?
IPA [u e l‿aʁɛ dø bys ||]

122

EN At the stoplight.

FR Au feu de circulation.
IPA [o fø dø siʁkylasjɔ̃ ||]

123

EN How old are your children?

FR Quel âge ont tes enfants?
IPA [kɛ l‿aʒ ɔ̃ te z‿ɑ̃fɑ̃ ||]

124

EN Five (5), seven (7), and ten (10).

FR Cinq, sept et dix ans.
IPA [sɛ̃k | sɛt e di z‿ɑ̃ ||]

125

EN How much are these oranges?

FR Combien coûtent ces oranges?
IPA [kɔ̃bjɛ̃ kut se z‿oʁɑ̃ʒ ‖]

126

EN A dollar fifty a pound ($1.50/lb). They're 2.3 Euros a kilo.

FR Deux euros trente le kilo.
IPA [dø z‿øʁo tʁɑ̃t lø kilo ‖]

127

EN What's your favorite sport?

FR Quel est ton sport favori?
IPA [kɛ l‿e tɔ̃ spɔʁ favoʁi ‖]

128

EN My favorite sport is skiing.

FR Mon sport favori est le ski.
IPA [mɔ̃ spɔʁ favoʁi e lø ski ‖]

129

EN Who's the man in this photo?

FR Qui est l'homme sur cette photo?
IPA [ki e l‿ɔm syʁ sɛt foto ‖]

130

EN That's my father.

FR C'est mon père.
IPA [sɛ mɔ̃ pɛʁ ||]

131

EN What color are your new shoes?

FR De quelle couleur sont tes nouvelles chaussures?
IPA [dø kɛl kulœʁ sɔ̃ te nuvɛl ʃosyʁ ||]

132

EN They're black.

FR Elles sont noires.
IPA [ɛl sɔ̃ nwaʁ ||]

133

EN What's your name?

FR Comment t'appelles-tu?
IPA [komã t‿apɛl ty ||]

134

EN I'm Brian.

FR Je m'appelle Brian.
IPA [ʒø m‿apɛl (...) ||]

135

EN Are you Australian?

FR Es-tu Australien?
IPA [ɛ ty ostʁaljɛ̃ ‖]

136

EN No, I'm Canadian.

FR Non, je suis Canadien.
IPA [nɔ̃ | ʒø sɥi kanadjɛ̃ ‖]

137

EN How old are you?

FR Quel âge as-tu?
IPA [kɛ l‿aʒ a ty ‖]

138

EN I'm thirty-three.

FR J'ai trente-trois ans.
IPA [ʒ‿ɛ tʁɑ̃ttʁwa z‿ɑ̃ ‖]

139

EN Are you a teacher?

FR Es-tu enseignant (♀enseignante)?
IPA [ɛ ty ɑ̃sɛɲɑ̃ (♀ɑ̃sɛɲɑ̃t) ‖]

140

EN No, I'm a doctor.

FR Non, je suis médecin.
IPA [nɔ̃ | ʒə sɥi mɛdsɛ̃ ||]

141

EN Are you married?

FR Es-tu marié (♀mariée)?
IPA [ɛ ty maʁje (♀maʁje) ||]

142

EN Yes, I am.

FR Oui, je le suis.
IPA [wi | ʒə lø sɥi ||]

143

EN Is your wife a doctor?

FR Ta femme est-elle médecin?
IPA [ta fam e t‿ɛl mɛdsɛ̃ ||]

144

EN No, she's a teacher.

FR Non, elle est enseignante.
IPA [nɔ̃ | ɛ l‿e t‿ãsɛɲãt ||]

145

EN Where is she from?

FR D'où vient-elle?
IPA [d̪u vjɛ̃ t̪ɛl |||]

146

EN She's from Mexico.

FR Elle vient du Mexique.
IPA [ɛl vjɛ̃ dø mɛksik |||]

147

EN What's her name?

FR Quel est son nom?
IPA [kɛ l̪e sɔ̃ nɔ̃ |||]

148

EN Her name is Barbara.

FR Elle s'appelle Barbara.
IPA [ɛl s̪apɛl (...) |||]

149

EN How old is she?

FR Quel âge a-t-elle?
IPA [kɛ l̪aʒ a t̪ɛl |||]

150

EN She's twenty-six (26).

FR Elle a vingt-six ans.
IPA [ɛ l̩a vɛ̃tsi z̃ɑ̃ ‖]

151

EN Are you married? — No, I'm not.

FR Es-tu marié (♀mariée)? — Non, je ne le suis pas.
IPA [ɛ ty maʁje (♀maʁje) ‖ — nɔ̃ | ʒø nø lø sɥi pa ‖]

152

EN Are you thirsty? — Yes, I am.

FR As-tu soif? — Oui, j'ai soif.
IPA [a ty swaf ‖ — wi | ʒ̩ɛ swaf ‖]

153

EN Is it cold today? — No, it isn't.

FR Fait-il froid aujourd'hui? — Non, il ne fait pas froid.
IPA [fɛ t̩il fʁwa oʒuʁdɥi ‖ — nɔ̃ | il nø fɛ pa fʁwa ‖]

154

EN Are your hands cold? — No, they aren't.

FR Tes mains sont-elles froides? — Non, elles ne le sont pas.
IPA [te mɛ̃ sɔ̃ t̩ɛl fʁwad ‖ — nɔ̃ | ɛl nø lø sɔ̃ pa ‖]

155

EN Is it dark now? — Yes, it is.

FR Fait-il noir maintenant? — Oui, il fait noir.
IPA [fɛ t il nwaʁ mɛ̃t°nã || — wi | il fɛ nwaʁ ||]

156

EN Are you a teacher? — Yes, I am.

FR Es-tu enseignant (♀enseignante)? — Oui, je le suis.
IPA [ɛ ty ãsɛɲã (♀ãsɛɲãt) || — wi | ʒø lø sɥi ||]

157

EN I'm working. I'm not watching TV.

FR Je suis en train de travailler. Je ne suis pas en train de regarder la télé.
IPA [ʒø sɥi z ã tʁɛ̃ dø tʁavaje || ʒø nø sɥi pa z ã tʁɛ̃ dø ʁ°gaʁde la tele ||]

158

EN Barbara is reading a newspaper.

FR Barbara lit le journal. > Barbara est en train de lire le journal.
IPA [(...) li lø ʒuʁnal || > (...) e t ã tʁɛ̃ dø liʁ lø ʒuʁnal ||]

159

EN She isn't eating.

FR Elle n'est pas en train de manger.
IPA [ɛl n̩e pa z̩ɑ̃ tʁɛ̃ dø mɑ̃ʒe ‖]

160

EN The phone is ringing.

FR Le téléphone sonne.
IPA [lø telefɔn sɔn ‖]

161

EN We're having dinner.

FR Nous dînons.
IPA [nu dinɔ̃ ‖]

162

EN You're not listening to me.

FR Tu ne m'écoutes pas.
IPA [ty nø m̩ekut pa ‖]

163

EN The children are doing their homework.

FR Les enfants sont en train de faire leurs devoirs.
IPA [le z̩ɑ̃fɑ̃ sɔ̃ t̩ɑ̃ tʁɛ̃ dø fɛʁ lœʁ d°vwaʁ ‖]

164

EN   Please be quiet. I'm working.

FR   Sois silencieux, s'il te plaît. Je travaille. > Silence, s'il te plaît. Je travaille.

IPA [swa silɑ̃sjø | s‿il tø plɛ || ʒø tʁavaj || > silɑ̃s | s‿il tø plɛ || ʒø tʁavaj ||]

165

EN   The weather's nice. It's not raining.

FR   Il faut beau. Il ne pleut pas.

IPA [il fo bo || il nø plø pa ||]

166

EN   Where are the children? — They're playing in the park.

FR   Où sont les enfants? — Ils jouent au parc.

IPA [u sɔ̃ le z‿ɑ̃fɑ̃ || — il ʒu o paʁk ||]

167

EN   We're having dinner now. Can I call you later?

FR   Nous sommes en train de dîner. Je peux te rappeler plus tard?

IPA [nu sɔm ɑ̃ tʁɛ̃ dø dine || ʒø pø tø ʁapəle plys taʁ ||]

168

EN I'm not watching TV.

FR Je ne regarde pas la télé.
IPA [ʒø nø ʁ°gaʁd pa la tele ‖]

169

EN She's eating an apple.

FR Elle mange une pomme.
IPA [ɛl mɑ̃ʒ yn pɔm ‖]

170

EN He's waiting for a bus.

FR Il attend un bus.
IPA [i l̯atɑ̃ d̯ œ̃ bys ‖]

171

EN They're playing football.

FR Ils (♀ elles) jouent au foot.
IPA [il (♀ ɛl) ʒu o fut ‖]

172

EN He's lying on the floor.

FR Il est couché sur le sol.
IPA [i l̯e kuʃe syʁ lø sɔl ‖]

173

EN We're eating breakfast.

FR Nous prenons le petit déjeuner.
IPA [nu pʁ°nɔ̃ lø p°ti deʒœne ‖]

174

EN She's sitting on the table.

FR Elle est assise sur la table.
IPA [ɛ l̩e t̩asiz syʁ la tabl ‖]

175

EN He's in the kitchen. He's cooking.

FR Il est dans la cuisine. Il cuisine.
IPA [i l̩e dɑ̃ la kɥizin ‖ il kɥizin ‖]

176

EN You stepped on my foot. — I'm sorry.

FR Tu m'as marché sur le pied. — Je suis désolé.
IPA [ty m̩a maʁʃe syʁ lø pje ‖ — ʒø sɥi dezole ‖]

177

EN Somebody is swimming in the river.

FR Quelqu'un nage dans la rivière.
IPA [kɛlkœ̃ naʒ dɑ̃ la ʁivjɛʁ ‖]

178

EN We're here on vacation. We're staying at a hotel on the beach.

FR Nous sommes en vacances. Nous séjournons dans un hôtel sur la plage.

IPA [nu sɔm ɑ̃ vakɑ̃s || nu seʒuʁnɔ̃ dɑ̃ z‿œ̃ n‿otɛl syʁ la plaʒ ||]

179

EN Where's Tara? — She's taking a shower.

FR Où est Tara? — Elle prend une douche.

IPA [u e (...) || — ɛl pʁɑ̃ d‿yn duʃ ||]

180

EN They're building a new hotel downtown.

FR Ils construisent un nouvel hôtel au centre-ville.

IPA [il kɔ̃stʁɥi z‿œ̃ nuvɛ l‿otɛl o sɑ̃tʁ°vil ||]

181

EN I'm leaving now, goodbye.

FR J'y vais maintenant, salut.

IPA [ʒ‿i vɛ mɛ̃t°nɑ̃ | saly ||]

182

EN She isn't having dinner.

FR Elle n'est pas en train de dîner.
IPA [ɛl n‿e pa z‿ɑ̃ tʁɛ̃ dø dine ‖]

183

EN She's watching TV.

FR Elle regarde la télé.
IPA [ɛl ʁ°gaʁd la tele ‖]

184

EN She's sitting on the floor.

FR Elle est assise sur le sol.
IPA [ɛ l‿e t‿asiz syʁ lø sɔl ‖]

185

EN She's reading a book.

FR Elle lit un livre.
IPA [ɛl li t‿œ̃ livʁ ‖]

186

EN He's not playing the piano.

FR Il n'est pas en train de jouer du piano.
IPA [il n‿e pa z‿ɑ̃ tʁɛ̃ dø ʒwe dy pjano ‖]

187

EN He's laughing.

FR Il rit.
IPA [il ʁi ‖]

188

EN He's wearing a hat.

FR Il porte un chapeau.
IPA [il pɔʁt œ̃ ʃapo ‖]

189

EN He's not writing a letter.

FR Il n'est pas en train d'écrire une lettre.
IPA [il n‿e pa z‿ɑ̃ tʁɛ̃ d‿ekʁiʁ yn lɛtʁ ‖]

190

EN I'm not washing my hair.

FR Je ne suis pas en train de me laver les cheveux.
IPA [ʒø nø sɥi pa z‿ɑ̃ tʁɛ̃ dø mø lave le ʃ°vø ‖]

191

EN It isn't snowing.

FR Il ne neige pas.
IPA [il nø nɛʒ pa ‖]

192

EN I'm sitting on a chair.

FR Je suis assis sur une chaise.
IPA [ʒø sɥi asi sy ʁ‿yn ʃɛz |||]

193

EN I'm not eating.

FR Je ne suis pas en train de manger.
IPA [ʒø nø sɥi pa z‿ɑ̃ tʁɛ̃ dø mɑ̃ʒe |||]

194

EN It's raining.

FR Il pleut.
IPA [il plø |||]

195

EN I'm not studying english.

FR Je ne suis pas en train d'étudier l'anglais.
IPA [ʒø nø sɥi pa z‿ɑ̃ tʁɛ̃ d‿etydje l‿ɑ̃glɛ |||]

196

EN I'm listening to music.

FR J'écoute de la musique.
IPA [ʒ‿ekut dø la myzik |||]

197

EN The sun isn't shining.

FR Le soleil ne brille pas.
IPA [lø solɛj nø bʁij pa ‖]

198

EN I'm wearing my shoes.

FR Je porte mes chaussures.
IPA [ʒø pɔʁt me ʃosyʁ ‖]

199

EN I'm not reading the newspaper.

FR Je ne suis pas en train de lire le journal.
IPA [ʒø nø sɥi pa z‿ɑ̃ tʁɛ̃ dø liʁ lø ʒuʁnal ‖]

200

EN Are you feeling okay?

FR Te sens-tu bien?
IPA [tø sɑ̃s ty bjɛ̃ ‖]

GMS #201 - 300

201

EN Yes, I'm fine.

FR Oui, je me sens bien.
IPA [wi | ʒø mø sãs bjɛ̃ ||]

202

EN Is it raining?

FR Est-ce qu'il pleut?
IPA [ɛs° k̩il plø ||]

203

EN Yes, take an umbrella.

FR Oui, prends un parapluie.
IPA [wi | pʁã z̩œ̃ paʁaplɥi ||]

204

EN Why are you wearing a coat?

FR Pourquoi portes-tu un manteau?
IPA [puʁkwa pɔʁt ty œ̃ mãto ||]

205

EN It's not cold.

FR Il ne fait pas froid.
IPA [il nø fɛ pa fʁwa ||]

206

EN What's he doing?

FR Que fait-il?
IPA [kø fɛ t‿il ||]

207

EN He's reading the newspaper.

FR Il lit le journal.
IPA [il li lø ʒuʁnal ||]

208

EN What are the children doing?

FR Que font les enfants?
IPA [kø fɔ̃ le z‿ãfã ||]

209

EN They're watching TV.

FR Ils regardent la télé.
IPA [il ʁ°gaʁd la tele ||]

210

EN Where's she going?

FR Où va-t-elle?
IPA [u va t‿ɛl ‖]

211

EN Who are you waiting for?

FR Qui attends-tu?
IPA [ki atɑ̃ ty ‖]

212

EN Are you waiting for John?

FR Attends-tu John?
IPA [atɑ̃ ty (...) ‖]

213

EN Are you leaving now?

FR Tu pars maintenant?
IPA [ty paʁ mɛ̃t°nɑ̃ ‖]

214

EN Yes, I am.

FR Oui, je pars maintenant.
IPA [wi | ʒø paʁ mɛ̃t°nɑ̃ ‖]

215

EN Is Chris working today?

FR Est-ce que Chris travaille aujourd'hui?
IPA [ɛsˠ kø (...) tʁavaj oʒuʁdɥi ||]

216

EN No, he isn't.

FR Non, il ne travaille pas aujourd'hui.
IPA [nɔ̃ | il nø tʁavaj pa z‿oʒuʁdɥi ||]

217

EN Is the sun shining?

FR Le soleil brille-t-il?
IPA [lø solɛj bʁij t‿il ||]

218

EN Yes, it is.

FR Oui, il brille.
IPA [wi | il bʁij ||]

219

EN Are your friends staying at a hotel?

FR Tes amis séjournent-ils à l'hôtel?
IPA [te z‿ami seʒuʁ n‿il a l‿otɛl ||]

220

EN No, they're staying with me.

FR Non, ils séjournent chez moi.
IPA [nɔ̃ | il seʒuʁn ʃe mwa ‖]

221

EN Are you watching TV?

FR Regardes-tu la télé?
IPA [ʁ°gaʁd ty la tele ‖]

222

EN No, you can turn it off.

FR Non, tu peux l'éteindre.
IPA [nɔ̃ | ty pø l̩etɛ̃dʁ ‖]

223

EN Are you leaving now?

FR Tu pars maintenant?
IPA [ty paʁ mɛ̃t°nɑ̃ ‖]

224

EN Yes, see you tomorrow.

FR Oui, on se voit demain.
IPA [wi | ɔ̃ sø vwa d°mɛ̃ ‖]

225

EN Is it raining?

FR Pleut-il?
IPA [plø t‿il ||]

226

EN No, not right now.

FR Non, pas maintenant.
IPA [nɔ̃ | pa mɛ̃t°nã ||]

227

EN Are you enjoying the movie?

FR Le film te plaît?
IPA [lø film tø plɛ ||]

228

EN Yes, it's very funny.

FR Oui, c'est vraiment drôle.
IPA [wi | sɛ vʁɛmã dʁol ||]

229

EN Does the clock work?

FR L'horloge fonctionne-t-elle?
IPA [l‿ɔʁlɔʒ fɔ̃ksjɔn t‿ɛl ||]

230

EN No, it's broken.

FR Non, elle est cassée.
IPA [nɔ̃ | ɛ l‿e kase ‖]

231

EN Are you waiting for a bus?

FR Tu attends un bus?
IPA [ty atɑ̃ z‿œ̃ bys ‖]

232

EN No, I'm waiting for a taxi.

FR Non, j'attends un taxi.
IPA [nɔ̃ | ʒ‿atɑ̃ œ̃ taksi ‖]

233

EN What are you reading?

FR Qu'est-ce que tu lis?
IPA [kɛsº kø ty lis ‖]

234

EN Where is she going?

FR Où va-t-elle?
IPA [u va t‿ɛl ‖]

235

EN What are you eating?

FR Qu'est-ce que tu manges?
IPA [kɛsᵊ kø ty mɑ̃ʒ ‖]

236

EN Why are you crying?

FR Pourquoi pleures-tu?
IPA [puʁkwa plœʁ ty ‖]

237

EN What are they looking at?

FR Qu'est-ce qu'ils regardent?
IPA [kɛsᵊ k‿il ʁᵊgaʁd ‖]

238

EN Why is he laughing?

FR Pourquoi rit-il?
IPA [puʁkwa ʁi t‿il ‖]

239

EN Are you listening to me?

FR M'écoutes-tu?
IPA [m‿ekut ty ‖]

240

EN Where are your friends going?

FR Où vont tes parents?
IPA [u vɔ̃ te paʁɑ̃ ‖]

241

EN Are your parents watching TV?

FR Tes parents regardent-ils la télé?
IPA [te paʁɑ̃ ʁ°gaʁ d̯il la tele ‖]

242

EN What's Claire cooking?

FR Qu'est-ce que Claire cuisine?
IPA [kɛs° kø (...) kɥizin ‖]

243

EN Why are you looking at me?

FR Pourquoi me regardes-tu?
IPA [puʁkwa mø ʁ°gaʁd ty ‖]

244

EN Is the bus coming?

FR Est-ce que l'autobus arrive?
IPA [ɛs° kø l̯otobys aʁiv ‖]

245

EN Are you watching TV?

FR Regardes-tu la télé?
IPA [ʁᵊgaʁd ty la tele ‖]

246

EN No, I'm not.

FR Non, je ne la regarde pas.
IPA [nɔ̃ | ʒø nø la ʁᵊgaʁd pa ‖]

247

EN Are you wearing a watch?

FR Portes-tu une montre?
IPA [pɔʁt ty yn mɔ̃tʁ ‖]

248

EN No, I'm not.

FR Non, je n'en porte pas.
IPA [nɔ̃ | ʒø n‿ã pɔʁt pa ‖]

249

EN Is he eating something?

FR Il est en train de manger quelque chose?
IPA [i l‿e t‿ã tʁɛ̃ dø mã ʒe kɛlk ʃoz ‖]

250

EN No, he isn't.

FR Non, il ne mange pas.
IPA [nɔ̃ | il nø mɑ̃ʒ pa ‖]

251

EN Is it raining?

FR Est-ce qu'il pleut?
IPA [ɛsᵊ k‿il plø ‖]

252

EN No, it isn't.

FR Non, il ne pleut pas.
IPA [nɔ̃ | il nø plø pa ‖]

253

EN Are you sitting on the floor?

FR Es-tu assis sur le sol?
IPA [ɛ ty asi syʁ lø sɔl ‖]

254

EN Yes, I am.

FR Oui, je le suis.
IPA [wi | ʒø lø sɥi ‖]

255

EN Are you feeling all right?

FR Est-ce que tu te sens bien?
IPA [ɛsˀ kø ty tø sɑ̃s bjɛ̃ ||]

256

EN No, I'm not.

FR Non, je ne me sens pas bien.
IPA [nɔ̃ | ʒø nø mø sɑ̃s pa bjɛ̃ ||]

257

EN They're looking at their books.

FR Ils regardent leurs livres.
IPA [il ʁˀgaʁd lœʁ livʁ ||]

258

EN They read a lot.

FR Ils lisent beaucoup.
IPA [il liz boku ||]

259

EN He's eating ice cream.

FR Il mange de la glace.
IPA [il mɑ̃ʒ dø la glas ||]

260

EN He likes ice cream.

FR Il aime la glace.
IPA [i l‿em la glas ‖]

261

EN I work in an office.

FR Je travaille dans un bureau.
IPA [ʒø tʁavaj dɑ̃ z‿œ̃ byʁo ‖]

262

EN My brother works in a bank.

FR Mon frère travaille dans une banque.
IPA [mɔ̃ fʁɛʁ tʁavaj dɑ̃ z‿yn bɑ̃k ‖]

263

EN She lives in New York.

FR Elle vit à New York.
IPA [ɛl vi a nuw jɔʁk ‖]

264

EN Her parents live in Chicago.

FR Ses parents habitent à Chicago.
IPA [se paʁɑ̃ abit a (...) ‖]

265

EN It rains a lot in the winter.

FR Il pleut beaucoup en hiver.
IPA [il plø boku p‿ɑ̃ n‿ivɛʁ ||]

266

EN Mike has lunch at home every day.

FR Mike déjeune à la maison tous les jours.
IPA [(...) deʒœn a la mɛzɔ̃ tu le ʒuʁ ||]

267

EN I like big cities.

FR J'aime les grandes villes.
IPA [ʒ‿em le gʁɑ̃d vil ||]

268

EN Your English is good.

FR Ton anglais est bon.
IPA [tɔ̃ n‿ɑ̃glɛ z‿e bɔ̃ ||]

269

EN You speak English very well.

FR Tu parles très bien anglais.
IPA [ty paʁl tʁɛ bjɛ̃ n‿ɑ̃glɛ ||]

270

EN Minoru works very hard.

FR Minoru travaille très fort.
IPA [(...) tʁavaj tʁɛ fɔʁ ‖]

271

EN He starts at seven thirty (7:30).

FR Il commence à sept heures trente (7 h 30).
IPA [il komɑ̃s a sɛ t‿œʁ tʁɑ̃t (7 h 30) ‖]

272

EN And he finishes at eight [o'clock] (8:00) at night.

FR Et il finit à vingt heures.
IPA [e il fini a vɛ̃ t‿œʁ ‖]

273

EN The earth goes around the sun.

FR La Terre tourne autour du Soleil.
IPA [la tɛʁ tuʁn otuʁ dy solɛj ‖]

274

EN We do a lot of different things in our free time.

FR Nous faisons beaucoup de choses différentes dans nos temps libres.
IPA [nu fᵊzɔ̃ boku dø ʃoz difeʁɑ̃t dɑ̃ no tɑ̃ libʁ ‖]

275
EN It costs a lot of money.

FR Ça coûte très cher.
IPA [sa kut tʁɛ ʃɛʁ ||]

276
EN She always goes to work early.

FR Elle se rend toujours tôt au travail.
IPA [ɛl sø ʁɑ̃ tuʒuʁ to o tʁavaj ||]

277
EN She always gets to work early.

FR Elle arrive toujours tôt au travail.
IPA [ɛ l̩ aʁiv tuʒuʁ to o tʁavaj ||]

278
EN We often sleep late on weekends.

FR Nous faisons souvent la grasse matinée les week-ends.
IPA [nu fᵊzɔ̃ suvɑ̃ la gʁas matine le wikɛnd ||]

279
EN Megumi usually plays tennis on Sundays.

FR Megumi a l'habitude de jouer au tennis le dimanche.
IPA [(...) a l̩ abityd dø ʒwe o tenis lø dimɑ̃ʃ ||]

280

EN I sometimes walk to work, but not often.

FR Je vais parfois au travail à pied, mais pas souvent.
IPA [ʒø vɛ paʁfwa o tʁavaj a pje | mɛ pa suvɑ̃ ||]

281

EN She reads.

FR Elle lit.
IPA [ɛl li ||]

282

EN He thinks.

FR Il pense.
IPA [il pɑ̃s ||]

283

EN It flies.

FR Il (♀elle) vole.
IPA [il (♀ɛl) vɔl ||]

284

EN He dances.

FR Il danse.
IPA [il dɑ̃s ||]

285

EN She has.

FR Elle a.
IPA [ɛ l‿a ||]

286

EN It finishes.

FR Il (♀elle) finit.
IPA [il (♀ɛl) fini ||]

287

EN He plays the piano.

FR Il joue du piano.
IPA [il ʒu dy pjano ||]

288

EN They live in a very big house.

FR Ils (♀elles) vivent dans une très grande maison.
IPA [il (♀ɛl) viv dɑ̃ z‿yn tʁɛ gʁɑ̃d mɛzɔ̃ ||]

289

EN She eats a lot of fruit.

FR Elle mange beaucoup de fruits.
IPA [ɛl mɑ̃ʒ boku də fʁɥi ||]

290

EN He plays tennis.

FR Il joue au tennis.
IPA [il ʒu o tenis ‖]

291

EN We go to the movies a lot.

FR Nous allons souvent au cinéma.
IPA [nu z‿alɔ̃ suvɑ̃ o sinema ‖]

292

EN He sleeps seven (7) hours a night.

FR Il dort sept heures par nuit.
IPA [il dɔʁ sɛ t‿œʁ paʁ nɥi ‖]

293

EN She speaks four (4) languages.

FR Elle parle quatre langues.
IPA [ɛl paʁl katʁ lɑ̃g ‖]

294

EN Banks usually open at nine (9:00) in the morning.

FR Les banques ouvrent généralement à neuf heures (9 h) du matin.
IPA [le bɑ̃k uvʁ ʒeneʁal°mɑ̃ a nœ v‿œʁ (9 h) dy matɛ̃ ‖]

295

EN The museum closes at five (5) in the afternoon.

FR Le musée ferme à dix-sept heures (17 h).

IPA [lø myze fɛʁm a disɛ t‿œʁ (17 h) ‖]

296

EN She's a teacher. She teaches math to children.

FR Elle est enseignante. Elle enseigne les mathématiques aux enfants.

IPA [ɛ l‿e t‿ɑ̃sɛɲɑ̃t ‖ ɛ l‿ɑ̃sɛɲ le matematik o z‿ɑ̃fɑ̃ ‖]

297

EN My job is very interesting. I meet a lot of people.

FR Mon travail est très intéressant. Je rencontre beaucoup de gens.

IPA [mɔ̃ tʁavaj e tʁɛ z‿ɛ̃teʁɛsɑ̃ ‖ ʒø ʁɑ̃kɔ̃tʁ boku dø ʒɑ̃ ‖]

298

EN His car is always dirty. He never cleans it.

FR Sa voiture est très sale. Il ne la lave jamais.

IPA [sa vwatyʁ e tʁɛ sal ‖ il nø la lav ʒamɛ ‖]

299

EN Food is expensive. It costs a lot of money.

FR La nourriture coûte cher. Elle coûte beaucoup d'argent.

IPA [la nuʁityʁ kut ʃɛʁ || ɛl kut boku d‿aʁʒã ||]

300

EN Shoes are expensive. They cost a lot of money.

FR Les chaussures coûtent cher. Elles coûtent beaucoup d'argent.

IPA [le ʃosyʁ kut ʃɛʁ || ɛl kut boku d‿aʁʒã ||]

GMS #301 - 400

301

EN Water boils at one hundred degrees (100°) Celsius.

FR L'eau bout à cent degrés Celsius.
IPA [l̯o bu a sã dᵊgʁe (...) ||]

302

EN We're good friends. I like her and she likes me.

FR Nous sommes de bons amis. Je l'aime bien et elle m'aime bien.
IPA [nu sɔm dø bɔ̃ z̯ami || ʒø l̯em bjɛ̃ n̯e ɛl m̯em bjɛ̃ ||]

303

EN She always arrives early.

FR Elle arrive toujours tôt.
IPA [ɛ l̯aʁiv tuʒuʁ to ||]

304

EN I never go to the movies alone.

FR Je ne vais jamais au cinéma seul (♀seule).
IPA [ʒø nø vɛ ʒamɛ o sinema sœl (♀sœl) ||]

305

EN She always works hard.

FR Elle travaille toujours très dur.
IPA [ɛl tʁavaj tuʒuʁ tʁɛ dyʁ ‖]

306

EN Children usually like chocolate.

FR Les enfants aiment généralement le chocolat.
IPA [le z̥ãfã ɛm ʒeneʁal°mã lø ʃokola ‖]

307

EN She always enjoys parties.

FR Elle aime toujours les fêtes.
IPA [ɛ l̥ɛm tuʒuʁ le fɛt ‖]

308

EN I often forget people's names.

FR J'oublie souvent le nom des gens.
IPA [ʒ̥ubli suvã lø nɔ̃ de ʒã ‖]

309

EN He never watches TV.

FR Il ne regarde jamais la télé.
IPA [il nø ʁ°gaʁd ʒamɛ la tele ‖]

310

EN We usually have dinner at six thirty (6:30).

FR Nous dînons généralement à dix-huit heures trente.
IPA [nu dinɔ̃ ʒeneʁalᵊmã a dizɥi tˬœʁ tʁãt ||]

311

EN She always wears nice clothes.

FR Elle porte toujours de beaux vêtements.
IPA [ɛl pɔʁt tuʒuʁ də bo vɛtᵊmã ||]

312

EN I usually watch TV in the evening.

FR Je regarde généralement la télé durant la soirée.
IPA [ʒø ʁᵊgaʁd ʒeneʁalᵊmã la tele dyʁã la swaʁe ||]

313

EN I never read in bed.

FR Je ne lis jamais au lit.
IPA [ʒø nø lis ʒamɛ o li ||]

314

EN I often get up before seven (7:00).

FR Je me lève souvent avant sept heures (7 h).
IPA [ʒø mø lɛv suvã tˬavã sɛ tˬœʁ (7 h) ||]

315

EN I always go to work by bus.

FR Je me rends toujours au travail en autobus.
IPA [ʒø mø ʁɑ̃ tuʒuʁ o tʁavaj ɑ̃ n‿otobys ‖]

316

EN I usually go to school by bus.

FR Je me rends généralement à l'école en autobus.
IPA [ʒø mø ʁɑ̃ ʒeneʁal°mɑ̃ a l‿ekɔl ɑ̃ n‿otobys ‖]

317

EN I always drink coffee in the morning.

FR Je bois toujours du café le matin.
IPA [ʒø bwa tuʒuʁ dy kafe lø matɛ̃ ‖]

318

EN She doesn't drink coffee.

FR Elle ne boit pas de café.
IPA [ɛl nø bwa pa dø kafe ‖]

319

EN He doesn't like his job.

FR Il n'aime pas son travail.
IPA [il n‿em pa sɔ̃ tʁavaj ‖]

320

EN I drink coffee, but I don't drink tea.

FR Je bois du café, mais je ne bois pas de thé.
IPA [ʒø bwa dy kafe | mɛ ʒø nø bwa pa dø te ||]

321

EN She drinks tea, but she doesn't drink coffee.

FR Elle boit du thé, mais elle ne boit pas de café.
IPA [ɛl bwa dy te | mɛ ɛl nø bwa pa dø kafe ||]

322

EN You don't work very hard.

FR Tu ne travailles pas très fort.
IPA [ty nø tʁavaj pa tʁɛ fɔʁ ||]

323

EN We don't watch TV very often.

FR Nous ne regardons pas la télé très souvent.
IPA [nu nø ʁᵊgaʁdɔ̃ pa la tele tʁɛ suvɑ̃ ||]

324

EN The weather is usually nice.

FR Il fait généralement beau.
IPA [il fɛ ʒeneʁalᵊmɑ̃ bo ||]

325

EN It doesn't rain very often.

FR Il ne pleut pas très souvent.
IPA [il nø plø pa tʁɛ suvɑ̃ ||]

326

EN They don't know many people.

FR Ils (♀ elles) ne connaissent pas beaucoup de gens.
IPA [il (♀ ɛl) nø konɛs pa boku dø ʒɑ̃ ||]

327

EN They don't have many friends.

FR Ils (♀ elles) n'ont pas beaucoup d'amis.
IPA [il (♀ ɛl) n‿ɔ̃ pa boku d‿ami ||]

328

EN I don't like football.

FR Je n'aime pas le football.
IPA [ʒø n‿ɛm pa lø futbɔl ||]

329

EN He doesn't like football.

FR Il n'aime pas le football.
IPA [il n‿ɛm pa lø futbɔl ||]

330

EN I don't like him, and he doesn't like me.

FR Je ne l'aime pas et il ne m'aime pas.
IPA [ʒø nø l̪ɛm pa z̪e il nø m̪ɛm pa ‖]

331

EN My car doesn't use much gas.

FR Ma voiture ne consomme pas beaucoup d'essence.
IPA [ma vwatyʁ nø kõsɔm pa boku d̪esɑ̃s ‖]

332

EN Sometimes he's late, but not often.

FR Il est parfois en retard, mais pas souvent.
IPA [i l̪e paʁfwa z̪ɑ̃ ʁ°taʁ | mɛ pa suvɑ̃ ‖]

333

EN I don't like to wash the car.

FR Je n'aime pas laver la voiture.
IPA [ʒø n̪ɛm pa lave la vwatyʁ ‖]

334

EN I don't do it very often.

FR Je ne la lave pas très souvent.
IPA [ʒø nø la lav pa tʁɛ suvɑ̃ ‖]

335

EN She speaks Spanish, but she doesn't speak Italian.

FR Elle parle espagnol, mais elle ne parle pas italien.
IPA [ɛl paʁl ɛspaɲɔl | mɛ ɛl nø paʁl pa z‿italjɛ̃ ||]

336

EN He doesn't do his job very well.

FR Il ne fait pas très bien son travail.
IPA [il nø fɛ pa tʁɛ bjɛ̃ sɔ̃ tʁavaj ||]

337

EN She doesn't usually have breakfast.

FR Elle ne prend généralement pas le petit déjeuner.
IPA [ɛl nø pʁɑ̃ ʒeneʁal°mɑ̃ pa lø p°ti deʒœne ||]

338

EN I don't play the piano very well.

FR Je ne joue pas très bien du piano.
IPA [ʒø nø ʒu pa tʁɛ bjɛ̃ dy pjano ||]

339

EN She doesn't play the piano very well.

FR Elle ne joue pas très bien du piano.
IPA [ɛl nø ʒu pa tʁɛ bjɛ̃ dy pjano ||]

340

EN They don't know my phone number.

FR Ils (♀elles) ne connaissent pas mon numéro de téléphone.
IPA [il (♀ɛl) nø kɔnɛs pa mɔ̃ nymeʁo dø telefɔn ‖]

341

EN We don't work very hard.

FR Nous ne travaillons pas très fort.
IPA [nu nø tʁavajɔ̃ pa tʁɛ fɔʁ ‖]

342

EN David doesn't have a car.

FR David n'a pas de voiture.
IPA [(...) n‿a pa dø vwatyʁ ‖]

343

EN You don't do the same thing every day.

FR Tu ne fais pas la même chose tous les jours.
IPA [ty nø fɛ pa la mɛm ʃoz tu le ʒuʁ ‖]

344

EN They like classical music.

FR Ils (♀elles) aiment la musique classique.
IPA [il (♀ɛl) ɛm la myzik klasik ‖]

345

EN She doesn't like jazz music.

FR Elle n'aime pas le jazz.
IPA [εl n‿εm pa lø dʒaz ‖]

346

EN I like rock and roll music.

FR J'aime le rock and roll.
IPA [ʒ‿εm lø ʁɔk (...) ʁɔl ‖]

347

EN They don't like boxing.

FR Ils (♀elles) n'aiment pas la boxe.
IPA [il (♀εl) n‿εm pa la bɔks ‖]

348

EN She doesn't like baseball.

FR Elle n'aime pas le baseball.
IPA [εl n‿εm pa lø bezbol ‖]

349

EN I like tennis.

FR J'aime le tennis.
IPA [ʒ‿εm lø tenis ‖]

350

EN They like horror movies.

FR Ils (♀ elles) aiment les films d'horreur.
IPA [il (♀ ɛl) ɛm le film d‿ɔʁœʁ ||]

351

EN She doesn't like action movies.

FR Elle n'aime pas les films d'action.
IPA [ɛl n‿ɛm pa le film d‿aksjɔ̃ ||]

352

EN I like romantic movies.

FR J'aime les films romantiques.
IPA [ʒ‿ɛm le film ʁomɑ̃tik ||]

353

EN I never watch TV.

FR Je ne regarde jamais la télé.
IPA [ʒø nø ʁ°gaʁd ʒamɛ la tele ||]

354

EN I don't watch TV very often.

FR Je ne regarde pas la télé très souvent.
IPA [ʒø nø ʁ°gaʁd pa la tele tʁɛ suvɑ̃ ||]

355

EN I don't like to go to bars very often.

FR Je n'aime pas aller dans les bars très souvent.

IPA [ʒø n‿ɛm pa z‿ale dɑ̃ le baʁ tʁɛ suvɑ̃ ||]

356

EN She likes to ride her bicycle every day.

FR Elle aime se promener à vélo tous les jours.

IPA [ɛ l‿ɛm sø pʁɔmne a velo tu le ʒuʁ ||]

357

EN They always like to eat in restaurants.

FR Ils (♀elles) aiment toujours manger au restaurant.

IPA [il (♀ɛl) ɛm tuʒuʁ mɑ̃ʒe o ʁɛstoʁɑ̃ ||]

358

EN I never like to travel by train.

FR Je n'aime jamais voyager en train.

IPA [ʒø n‿ɛm ʒamɛ vwajaʒe ʁ‿ɑ̃ tʁɛ̃ ||]

359

EN I get the news every day, but sometimes I don't read it.

FR Je reçois les nouvelles tous les jours, mais parfois je ne les lis pas.

IPA [ʒø ʁ°swa le nuvɛl tu le ʒuʁ | mɛ paʁfwa ʒø nø le lis pa ||]

360

EN He has a car, but he doesn't use it very often.

FR Il a une voiture, mais il ne l'utilise pas très souvent.

IPA [i l̯a yn vwatyʁ | mɛ il nø l̯ytiliz pa tʁɛ suvɑ̃ ||]

361

EN His friends like the movies, but they usually watch movies at home.

FR Ses amis (♀amies) aiment aller au cinéma, mais ils (♀elles) regardent généralement des films à la maison.

IPA [se z̯ami (♀ami) ɛm ale o sinema | mɛ il (♀ɛl) ʁ°gaʁd ʒeneʁal°mɑ̃ de film a la mɛzɔ̃ ||]

362

EN She's married, but she doesn't wear a ring.

FR Elle est mariée, mais elle ne porte pas d'anneau.

IPA [ɛ l̯e maʁje | mɛ ɛl nø pɔʁt pa d̯ano ||]

363

EN I don't know much about politics. I'm not interested in it.

FR Je ne connais pas grand-chose à la politique. Ça ne m'intéresse pas beaucoup.

IPA [ʒø nø konɛ pa gʁɑ̃ʃoz a la politik || sa nø m‿ɛ̃teʁɛs pa boku |||]

364

EN This hotel isn't expensive. It doesn't cost much to stay there.

FR Cet hôtel ne coûte pas cher. Ça ne coûte pas beaucoup d'argent d'y séjourner.

IPA [sɛ t‿otɛl nø kut pa ʃɛʁ || sa nø kut pa boku d‿aʁʒɑ̃ d‿i seʒuʁne |||]

365

EN He lives near us, but we don't see him very often.

FR Il habite près de chez nous, mais nous ne le voyons pas souvent.

IPA [i l‿abit pʁɛ dø ʃe nu | mɛ nu nø lø vwajɔ̃ pa suvɑ̃ |||]

366

EN She speaks four (4) languages.

FR Elle parle quatre langues.

IPA [ɛl paʁl katʁ lɑ̃g |||]

367
EN I don't like my job. It's very boring.

FR Je n'aime pas mon travail. C'est très ennuyant.
IPA [ʒø n‿ɛm pa mɔ̃ tʁavaj || sɛ tʁɛ z‿ɑ̃nɥijɑ̃ ||]

368
EN Where is he? — I'm sorry, I don't know.

FR Où est-il? — Je suis désolé, je ne sais pas.
IPA [u e t‿il || — ʒø sɥi dezole | ʒø nø sɛ pa ||]

369
EN She's a very quiet person. She doesn't talk very much.

FR C'est une personne très silencieuse. Elle ne parle pas beaucoup.
IPA [sɛ t‿yn pɛʁsɔn tʁɛ silɑ̃sjøz || ɛl nø paʁl pa boku ||]

370
EN He drinks a lot of coffee. It's his favorite drink.

FR Il boit beaucoup de café. C'est son breuvage favori.
IPA [il bwa boku dø kafe || sɛ sɔ̃ bʁœvaʒ favoʁi ||]

371
EN It's not true. I don't believe it.

FR Ce n'est pas vrai. Je n'y crois pas.
IPA [sø n‿e pa vʁɛ || ʒø n‿i kʁwa pa ||]

372

EN That's a very beautiful picture. I like it a lot.

FR C'est une très belle photo. Je l'aime beaucoup.
IPA [sɛ t‿yn tʁɛ bɛl foto || ʒø l‿ɛm boku ||]

373

EN He's a vegetarian. He doesn't eat meat.

FR Il est végétarien. Il ne mange pas de viande.
IPA [i l‿e veʒetaʁjɛ̃ || il nø mɑ̃ʒ pa dø vjɑ̃d ||]

374

EN Do you work on Sunday?

FR Travailles-tu les dimanches?
IPA [tʁavaj ty le dimɑ̃ʃ ||]

375

EN Do your friends live near here?

FR Est-ce que tes amis (♀ amies) vivent près d'ici?
IPA [ɛsᵊ kø te z‿ami (♀ ami) viv pʁɛ d‿isi ||]

376

EN Does Emily play tennis?

FR Est-ce qu'Emily joue au tennis?
IPA [ɛsᵊ k (...) ʒu o tenis ||]

377

EN Where do your parents live?

FR Où vivent tes parents?
IPA [u viv te paʁɑ̃ ||]

378

EN How often do you wash your hair?

FR À quelle fréquence te laves-tu les cheveux?
IPA [a kɛl fʁekɑ̃s tø lav ty le ʃ°vø ||]

379

EN What does this word mean?

FR Qu'est-ce que ce mot signifie?
IPA [kɛs° kø sø mo siɲifi ||]

380

EN How much does it cost to fly to New York?

FR Combien coûte un vol pour New York?
IPA [kɔ̃bjɛ̃ kut œ̃ vɔl puʁ nuw jɔʁk ||]

381

EN Do you always have breakfast?

FR Déjeunes-tu tous les matins?
IPA [deʒœn ty tu le matɛ̃ ||]

382

EN Does Wenjie ever call you?

FR Est-ce que Wenjie t'appelle parfois?
IPA [ɛsᵊ kø (...) t‿apɛl paʁfwa ‖]

383

EN What do you usually do on weekends?

FR Que fais-tu d'habitude les week-ends?
IPA [kø fɛ ty d‿abityd le wikɛnd ‖]

384

EN Do they like music?

FR Aiment-ils (♀elles) la musique?
IPA [ɛ m‿il (♀ɛl) la myzik ‖]

385

EN Does he like music?

FR Aime-t-il la musique?
IPA [ɛm t‿il la myzik ‖]

386

EN Do your parents speak English?

FR Est-ce que tes parents parlent anglais?
IPA [ɛsᵊ kø te paʁɑ̃ paʁl ɑ̃glɛ ‖]

387

EN Does your father work hard?

FR Est-ce que ton père travaille fort?
IPA [ɛsˤ kø tɔ̃ pɛʁ tʁavaj fɔʁ ‖]

388

EN Does your sister live in Canada?

FR Est-ce que ta sœur habite au Canada?
IPA [ɛsˤ kø ta sœʁ abit o kanada ‖]

389

EN I like chocolate. How about you? Do you like chocolate?

FR J'aime le chocolat. Et toi? Aimes-tu le chocolat?
IPA [ʒ‿em lø ʃokola ‖ e twa ‖ em ty lø ʃokola ‖]

390

EN I play tennis. How about you? Do you play tennis?

FR Je joue au tennis. Et toi? Joues-tu au tennis?
IPA [ʒø ʒu o tenis ‖ e twa ‖ ʒu ty o tenis ‖]

391

EN You live near here. How about Fred? Does he live near here?

FR Tu habites près d'ici. Fred, lui? Il habite près d'ici?
IPA [ty abit pʁɛ d‿isi ‖ (...) ‖ lɥi ‖ i l‿abit pʁɛ d‿isi ‖]

392

EN Jisang plays tennis. How about his friends? Do they play tennis?

FR Jisang joue au tennis. Ses amis, eux? (♀ Ses amies, elles?) Jouent-ils au tennis? (♀ Jouent-elles au tennis?)

IPA [(...) ʒu o tenis || se z‿ami | ø || (♀ se z‿ami | ɛl ||) ʒu t‿il o tenis || (♀ ʒu t‿ɛl o tenis ||)]

393

EN You speak English. How about your brother? Does he speak English?

FR Tu parles anglais. Ton frère, lui? Parle-t-il anglais?

IPA [ty paʁl ɑ̃glɛ || tɔ̃ fʁɛʁ | lɥi || paʁl t‿il ɑ̃glɛ ||]

394

EN I do yoga every morning. How about you? Do you do yoga every morning?

FR Je fais du yoga tous les matins. Et toi? Fais-tu du yoga tous les matins?

IPA [ʒø fɛ dy joga tu le matɛ̃ || e twa || fɛ ty dy joga tu le matɛ̃ ||]

395

EN Yaqin often travels on business. How about Gary? Does he often travel on business?

FR Yaqin voyage souvent pour affaires. Gary, lui? Voyage-t-il souvent pour affaires?

IPA [(...) vwajaʒ suvã pu ʁ‿afɛʁ || (...) | lɥi || vwajaʒ t‿il suvã pu ʁ‿afɛʁ ||]

396

EN I want to be famous. How about you? Do you want to be famous?

FR Je veux être célèbre. Et toi? Veux-tu être célèbre?

IPA [ʒø vø ɛtʁ selɛbʁ || e twa || vø ty ɛtʁ selɛbʁ ||]

397

EN You work hard. How about Heuiyeon? Does she work hard?

FR Tu travailles fort. Heuiyeon, elle? Travaille-t-elle fort?

IPA [ty tʁavaj fɔʁ || (...) | ɛl || tʁavaj t‿ɛl fɔʁ ||]

398

EN Where do your parents live?

FR Où tes parents habitent-ils?

IPA [u te paʁã abi t‿il ||]

399

EN Do you always get up early?

FR Te lèves-tu toujours tôt?
IPA [tø lɛv ty tuʒuʁ to ‖]

400

EN How often do you watch TV?

FR À quelle fréquence regardes-tu la télé?
IPA [a kɛl fʁekɑ̃s ʁᵊgaʁd ty la tele ‖]

GMS #401 - 500

401

EN What do you want for dinner?

FR Qu'est-ce que tu veux pour dîner?
IPA [kɛsᵊ kø ty vø puʁ dine ‖]

402

EN Do you like football?

FR Aimes-tu le football?
IPA [ɛm ty lø futbɔl ‖]

403

EN Does your brother like football?

FR Est-ce que ton frère aime le football?
IPA [ɛsᵊ kø tɔ̃ fʁɛʁ ɛm lø futbɔl ‖]

404

EN What do you do in your free time?

FR Que fais-tu dans tes temps libres?
IPA [kø fɛ ty dɑ̃ te tɑ̃ libʁ ‖]

405

EN Where does your sister work?

FR Ta sœur travaille à quel endroit?
IPA [ta sœʁ tʁavaj a kɛ l ãdʁwa ‖]

406

EN Do you ever go to the movies?

FR Vas-tu parfois au cinéma?
IPA [va ty paʁfwa o sinema ‖]

407

EN What does this word mean?

FR Qu'est-ce que ce mot signifie?
IPA [kɛsᵊ kø sø mo siɲifi ‖]

408

EN How often does it snow here?

FR À quelle fréquence neige-t-il ici?
IPA [a kɛl fʁekãs nɛʒ t̯il isi ‖]

409

EN What time do you usually go to bed?

FR À quelle heure vas-tu généralement au lit?
IPA [a kɛ l̯œʁ va ty ʒeneʁalᵊmã o li ‖]

410

EN How much does it cost to call Mexico?

FR Combien coûte un appel au Mexique?
IPA [kɔ̃bjɛ̃ kut œ̃ n‿apɛl o meksik ‖]

411

EN What do you usually have for breakfast?

FR Que manges-tu généralement pour le petit déjeuner?
IPA [kø mɑ̃ʒ ty ʒeneʁalᵊmɑ̃ puʁ lø pᵊti deʒœne ‖]

412

EN Do you watch TV a lot? — No, I don't.

FR Regardes-tu souvent la télé? — Non, je ne regarde
pas la télé souvent.
IPA [ʁᵊgaʁd ty suvɑ̃ la tele ‖ — nɔ̃ | ʒø nø ʁᵊgaʁd pa la
tele suvɑ̃ ‖]

413

EN Do you live in a big city? — No, I don't.

FR Vis-tu dans une grande ville? — Non, je ne vis pas
dans une grande ville.
IPA [vis ty dɑ̃ z‿yn gʁɑ̃d vil ‖ — nɔ̃ | ʒø nø vis pa dɑ̃
z‿yn gʁɑ̃d vil ‖]

414

EN Do you ever ride a bicycle? — Not usually.

FR Te promènes-tu parfois à vélo? — Non, pas souvent.

IPA [tø pʁomɛn ty paʁfwa a velo || — nɔ̃ | pa suvã ||]

415

EN Does it rain a lot where you live? — Not much.

FR Est-ce qu'il pleut beaucoup où tu habites? — Non, pas beaucoup.

IPA [ɛsᵊ k‿il plø boku p‿u ty abit || — nɔ̃ | pa boku ||]

416

EN Do you play the piano? — No, I don't.

FR Joues-tu du piano? — Non, je ne joue pas du piano.

IPA [ʒu ty dy pjano || — nɔ̃ | ʒø nø ʒu pa dy pjano ||]

417

EN Zhirong's watching television.

FR Zhirong regarde la télé.

IPA [(...) ʁᵊgaʁd la tele ||]

418

EN He's not playing the guitar.

FR Il ne joue pas de la guitare.

IPA [il nø ʒu pa dø la gitaʁ ||]

419

EN But Zhirong has a guitar.

FR Mais Zhirong a une guitare.
IPA [mɛ (...) a yn gitaʁ ||]

420

EN He plays guitar a lot, and he plays very well.

FR Il joue souvent de la guitare et il joue très bien.
IPA [il ʒu suvã dø la gitaʁ e il ʒu tʁɛ bjẽ ||]

421

EN Zhirong plays the guitar.

FR Zhirong joue de la guitare.
IPA [(...) ʒu dø la gitaʁ ||]

422

EN But he's not playing the guitar now.

FR Mais il ne joue pas de la guitare en ce moment.
IPA [mɛ il nø ʒu pa dø la gitaʁ ã sø momã ||]

423

EN Is Zhirong playing the guitar? — No, he isn't.

FR Zhirong joue-t-il de la guitare en ce moment? — Non, il ne joue pas de la guitare en ce moment.
IPA [(...) ʒu t‿il dø la gitaʁ ã sø momã || — nõ | il nø ʒu pa dø la gitaʁ ã sø momã ||]

424

EN Does he play the guitar? — Yes, he does.

FR Joue-t-il de la guitare? — Oui, il joue de la guitare.
IPA [ʒu t‿il də la gitaʁ || — wi | il ʒu də la gitaʁ ||]

425

EN Please be quiet. I'm working.

FR Silence, s'il vous plaît. Je travaille.
IPA [silɑ̃s | s‿il vu plɛ || ʒø tʁavaj ||]

426

EN Yiting's taking a shower at the moment.

FR Yiting prend une douche en ce moment.
IPA [(...) pʁɑ̃ d‿yn duʃ ɑ̃ sø momɑ̃ ||]

427

EN Take an umbrella with you. It's raining.

FR Prends un parapluie. Il pleut.
IPA [pʁɑ̃ z‿œ̃ paʁaplɥi || il plø ||]

428

EN You can turn off the TV. I'm not watching it.

FR Tu peux éteindre la télé. Je ne la regarde pas.
IPA [ty pø etɛ̃dʁ la tele || ʒø nø la ʁᵊgaʁd pa ||]

429

EN   Why are you under the table? What are you doing?

FR   Pourquoi es-tu sous la table? Qu'est-ce que tu fais?

IPA   [puʁkwa ɛ ty su la tabl || kɛsə kø ty fɛ ||]

430

EN   I work every day from nine (9:00) to five-thirty (5:30).

FR   Je travaille tous les jours de neuf heures (9 h) à dix-sept heures trente (17 h 30).

IPA   [ʒø tʁavaj tu le ʒuʁ dø nœ v‿œʁ (9 h) a disɛ t‿œʁ tʁɑ̃t (17 h 30) ||]

431

EN   Howard takes a shower every morning.

FR   Howard prend une douche tous les matins.

IPA   [(...) pʁɑ̃ d‿yn duʃ tu le matɛ̃ ||]

432

EN   It rains a lot in the winter.

FR   Il pleut beaucoup en hiver.

IPA   [il plø boku p‿ɑ̃ n‿ivɛʁ ||]

433

EN I don't watch TV very often.

FR Je ne regarde pas la télé très souvent.
IPA [ʒø nø ʁˀgaʁd pa la tele tʁɛ suvã ‖]

434

EN What do you usually do on weekends?

FR Que fais-tu généralement les week-ends?
IPA [kø fɛ ty ʒeneʁalˀmã le wikɛnd ‖]

435

EN Do you like her?

FR Tu l'aimes bien?
IPA [ty l‿ɛm bjɛ̃ ‖]

436

EN Do you love her?

FR Tu l'aimes?
IPA [ty l‿ɛm ‖]

437

EN Do you want to know the answer?

FR Veux-tu savoir la réponse?
IPA [vø ty savwaʁ la ʁepɔ̃s ‖]

438

EN Do you understand me?

FR Est-ce que tu me comprends?
IPA [ɛsᵊ kø ty mø kɔ̃pʁɑ̃ ||]

439

EN Do you remember that day?

FR Te souviens-tu de ce jour?
IPA [tø suvjɛ̃ ty dø sø ʒuʁ ||]

440

EN It depends on you.

FR Ça dépend de toi.
IPA [sa depɑ̃ dø twa ||]

441

EN What do you prefer?

FR Qu'est-ce que tu préfères?
IPA [kɛsᵊ kø ty pʁefɛʁ ||]

442

EN Do you hate me?

FR Est-ce que tu me hais?
IPA [ɛsᵊ kø ty mø ɛ ||]

443

EN What do you need?

FR De quoi as-tu besoin?
IPA [dø kwa a ty bøzwɛ̃ ||]

444

EN What do you mean?

FR Qu'est-ce que tu veux dire?
IPA [kɛsˀ kø ty vø diʁ ||]

445

EN Do you believe me?

FR Me crois-tu?
IPA [mø kʁwa ty ||]

446

EN I don't believe you.

FR Je ne te crois pas.
IPA [ʒø nø tø kʁwa pa ||]

447

EN Do you forget the answer?

FR Tu oublies la réponse?
IPA [ty ubli la ʁepɔ̃s ||]

448

EN Does he take photographs?

FR Prend-il des photos?
IPA [pʁɑ̃ d͜ il de foto ‖]

449

EN Is he taking a photograph?

FR Est-il en train de prendre une photo?
IPA [e t͜ il ɑ̃ tʁɛ̃ dø pʁɑ̃dʁ yn foto ‖]

450

EN What's he doing now?

FR Que fait-il en ce moment?
IPA [kø fɛ t͜ il ɑ̃ sø momɑ̃ ‖]

451

EN Is she driving a bus?

FR Est-elle en train de conduire un autobus?
IPA [e t͜ ɛl ɑ̃ tʁɛ̃ dø kɔ̃dɥiʁ œ̃ n͜ otobys ‖]

452

EN Does she drive a bus?

FR Conduit-elle un autobus?
IPA [kɔ̃dɥi t͜ ɛl œ̃ n͜ otobys ‖]

453

EN What's she doing now?

FR Que fait-elle en ce moment?
IPA [kø fɛ t̪ɛl ɑ̃ sø momɑ̃ ||]

454

EN Does he wash windows?

FR Lave-t-il des vitres?
IPA [lav t̪il de vitʁ ||]

455

EN Is he washing a window?

FR Est-il en train de laver une vitre?
IPA [e t̪il ɑ̃ tʁɛ̃ dø lave ʁ̯yn vitʁ ||]

456

EN What's he doing now?

FR Que fait-il en ce moment?
IPA [kø fɛ t̪il ɑ̃ sø momɑ̃ ||]

457

EN Are they teaching?

FR Est-ce qu'ils (♀elles) sont en train d'enseigner?
IPA [ɛsə k̯il (♀ɛl) sɔ̃ t̪ɑ̃ tʁɛ̃ d̪ɑ̃seɲe ||]

458

EN Do they teach?

FR Enseignent-ils (♀ elles)?
IPA [ãsɛɲ t̪il (♀ ɛl) ‖]

459

EN What do they do?

FR Que font-ils (♀ elles)?
IPA [kø fɔ̃ t̪il (♀ ɛl) ‖]

460

EN Excuse me, do you speak English?

FR Pardon, parlez-vous anglais?
IPA [paʁdɔ̃ | paʁle vu ãglɛ ‖]

461

EN Where's Kelly? — I don't know.

FR Où est Kelly? — Je ne sais pas.
IPA [u e (...) ‖ — ʒø nø sɛ pa ‖]

462

EN What's so funny? Why are you laughing?

FR Qu'est-ce qui est si drôle? Pourquoi ris-tu?
IPA [kɛsᵊ ki e si dʁol ‖ puʁkwa ʁi ty ‖]

463

EN What does your sister do? — She's a dentist.

FR Ta sœur fait quoi comme travail? — Elle est dentiste.
IPA [ta sœʁ fɛ kwa kɔm tʁavaj || — ɛ l̩e dɑ̃tist ||]

464

EN It's raining. I don't want to go out in the rain.

FR Il pleut. Je ne veux pas sortir sous la pluie.
IPA [il plø || ʒø nø vø pa sɔʁtiʁ su la plɥi ||]

465

EN Where do you come from?

FR D'où viens-tu?
IPA [d̩u vjɛ̃ ty ||]

466

EN How much does it cost to send a package to Canada?

FR Combien coûte l'envoi d'un paquet au Canada?
IPA [kɔ̃bjɛ̃ kut l̩ɑ̃vwa d̩œ̃ pakɛ o kanada ||]

467

EN He's a good tennis player, but he doesn't play very often.

FR C'est un bon joueur de tennis, mais il ne joue pas très souvent.
IPA [sɛ t̩œ̃ bɔ̃ ʒwœʁ dø tenis | mɛ il nø ʒu pa tʁɛ suvɑ̃ ||]

468

EN Where's Jirou? — He's taking a shower.

FR Où est Jirou? — Il prend une douche.
IPA [u e (...) || — il pʁɑ̃ d‿yn duʃ ||]

469

EN I don't watch TV very often.

FR Je ne regarde pas la télé très souvent.
IPA [ʒø nø ʁ°gaʁd pa la tele tʁɛ suvɑ̃ ||]

470

EN Somebody's singing.

FR Quelqu'un chante.
IPA [kɛlkœ̃ ʃɑ̃t ||]

471

EN Junko's tired. She wants to go home now.

FR Junko est fatiguée. Elle veut rentrer à la maison maintenant.
IPA [(...) e fatige || ɛl vø ʁɑ̃tʁe a la mɛzɔ̃ mɛ̃t°nɑ̃ ||]

472

EN How often do you read the news?

FR À quelle fréquence lis-tu les nouvelles?
IPA [a kɛl fʁekɑ̃s lis ty le nuvɛl ||]

473

EN Excuse me, but you're sitting in my seat. — I'm sorry.

FR Excusez-moi, vous êtes assis dans mon siège. — Je suis désolé.

IPA [ɛkskyze mwa | vu z̯ɛt asi dɑ̃ mɔ̃ sjɛʒ || — ʒø sɥi dezole ||]

474

EN I'm sorry, I don't understand. Can you speak more slowly?

FR Je suis désolé, je ne comprends pas. Peux-tu parler plus lentement?

IPA [ʒø sɥi dezole | ʒø nø kɔ̃pʁɑ̃ pa || pø ty paʁle plys lɑ̃t°mɑ̃ ||]

475

EN It's late. I'm going home now. Are you coming with me?

FR Il est tard. Je rentre à la maison. Viens-tu avec moi?

IPA [i l̯e taʁ || ʒø ʁɑ̃tʁ a la mɛzɔ̃ || vjɛ̃ ty avɛk mwa ||]

476

EN What time does your father finish work every day?

FR À quelle heure ton père finit-il de travailler chaque jour?

IPA [a kɛ l̯œʁ tɔ̃ pɛʁ fini t̯il dø tʁavaje ʃak ʒuʁ ||]

477

EN You can turn the music off. I'm not listening to it.

FR Tu peux éteindre la musique. Je ne l'écoute pas.
IPA [ty pø etɛ̃dʁ la myzik || ʒø nø l̩ekut pa ||]

478

EN He's in the kitchen cooking something.

FR Il est dans la cuisine, en train de cuisiner quelque
chose.
IPA [i l̩e dã la kɥizin | ã tʁɛ̃ dø kɥizine kɛlk ʃoz ||]

479

EN Jack doesn't usually drive to work. He usually walks.

FR Jack ne se rend généralement pas au travail en
voiture. Il a l'habitude de marcher.
IPA [(...) nø sø ʁã ʒeneʁalᵊmã pa o tʁavaj ã vwatyʁ || i
l̩a l̩abityd dø maʁʃe ||]

480

EN Lucy doesn't like coffee. She prefers tea.

FR Lucie n'aime pas le café. Elle préfère le thé.
IPA [lusi n̩ɛm pa lø kafe || ɛl pʁefɛʁ lø te ||]

481

EN I have blue eyes. > I've got blue eyes.

FR J'ai les yeux bleus.
IPA [ʒ‿ɛ le z‿jø blø ‖]

482

EN Ganesh has two (2) sisters. > Ganesh's got two (2) sisters.

FR Ganesh a deux sœurs.
IPA [(...) a dø sœʁ ‖]

483

EN Our car has four (4) doors. > Our car's got four (4) doors.

FR Notre voiture a quatre portes.
IPA [nɔtʁ vwatyʁ a katʁ pɔʁt ‖]

484

EN She isn't feeling well. She has a headache. > She's got a headache.

FR Elle ne se sent pas bien. Elle a mal à la tête.
IPA [ɛl nø sø sɑ̃ pa bjɛ̃ ‖ ɛ l‿a mal a la tɛt ‖]

485

EN They like animals. They have a horse, three (3) dogs, and six (6) cats. They've got a lot of animals.

FR Ils (♀elles) aiment les animaux. Ils (♀elles) ont un cheval, trois chiens et six chats. Ils (♀elles) ont beaucoup d'animaux.

IPA [il (♀ɛl) ɛm le z‿animo || il (♀ɛl) ɔ̃ t‿œ ʃ°val | tʁwa ʃjɛ̃ e sis ʃa || il (♀ɛl) ɔ̃ boku d‿animo ||]

486

EN I have a bike, but I don't have a car. > I've got a bike, but I haven't got a car.

FR J'ai un vélo, mais je n'ai pas de voiture.

IPA [ʒ‿ɛ œ̃ velo | mɛ ʒø n‿ɛ pa dø vwatyʁ ||]

487

EN They don't have any children. > They haven't got any children.

FR Ils (♀elles) n'ont pas d'enfants.

IPA [il (♀ɛl) n‿ɔ̃ pa d‿ɑ̃fɑ̃ ||]

488

EN It's a nice house, but it doesn't have a garage. > It hasn't got a garage.

FR C'est une belle maison, mais elle n'a pas de garage.

IPA [sɛ t‿yn bɛl mɛzɔ̃ | mɛ ɛl n‿a pa dø gaʁaʒ ||]

489

EN Lila doesn't have a job. > Lila hasn't got a job.

FR Lila n'a pas de travail.
IPA [(...) n‿a pa də tʁavaj ‖]

490

EN Does your phone have a camera?

FR Ton portable a-t-il une caméra? > Est-ce que ton portable a une caméra?
IPA [tɔ̃ pɔʁtabl a t‿il yn kameʁa ‖ > ɛsᵊ kø tɔ̃ pɔʁtabl a yn kameʁa ‖]

491

EN Does Nicole have a car? > Has Nicole got a car?

FR Est-ce que Nicole a une voiture? > Nicole a-t-elle une voiture?
IPA [ɛsᵊ kø (...) a yn vwatyʁ ‖ > (...) a t‿ɛl yn vwatyʁ ‖]

492

EN What kind of car does she have? > What kind of car has she got?

FR Quelle sorte de voiture a-t-elle?
IPA [kɛl sɔʁt də vwatyʁ a t‿ɛl ‖]

493

EN What do you have in your bag? > What have you got in your bag?

FR Qu'est-ce que tu as dans ton sac?
IPA [kɛsᵊ kø ty a dɑ̃ tɔ̃ sak ‖]

494

EN Do you have a camera? — No, I don't.

FR As-tu une caméra? — Non, je n'en ai pas.
IPA [a ty yn kameʁa ‖ — nɔ̃ | ʒø n̪ɑ̃ ɛ pa ‖]

495

EN Have you got a camera? — No, I don't.

FR As-tu une caméra? — Non, je n'en ai pas.
IPA [a ty yn kameʁa ‖ — nɔ̃ | ʒø n̪ɑ̃ ɛ pa ‖]

496

EN Does she have a car? — No, she doesn't.

FR A-t-elle une voiture? — Non, elle n'en a pas.
IPA [a t̪ɛl yn vwatyʁ ‖ — nɔ̃ | ɛl n̪ɑ̃ a pa ‖]

497

EN Ask if he has a computer. — Yes, he's got a computer.

FR Demande s'il a un ordinateur. — Oui, il en a un.
IPA [dᵊmɑ̃d s̪il a œ̃ n̪ɔʁdinatœʁ ‖ — wi | i l̪ɑ̃ n̪a œ̃ ‖]

498

EN Ask if he has a dog. — No, he hasn't got a dog.

FR Demande s'il a un chien. — Non, il n'en a pas.
IPA [dᵊmɑ̃d s‿il a œ̃ ʃjɛ̃ ‖ — nɔ̃ | il n‿ɑ̃ a pa ‖]

499

EN Ask if he has a smart phone. — No, he hasn't got a smart phone.

FR Demande s'il a un téléphone intelligent. — Non, il n'en a pas.
IPA [dᵊmɑ̃d s‿il a œ̃ telefɔn ɛ̃teliʒɑ̃ ‖ — nɔ̃ | il n‿ɑ̃ a pa ‖]

500

EN Ask if he has a watch. — Yes, he's got a watch.

FR Demande s'il a une montre. — Oui, il en a une.
IPA [dᵊmɑ̃d s‿il a yn mɔ̃tʁ ‖ — wi | i l‿ɑ̃ n‿a yn ‖]

GMS #501 - 600

501

EN Ask if he has any brothers or sisters. — Yes, he's got a brother and two (2) sisters.

FR Demande s'il a des frères et sœurs. — Oui, il a un frère et deux soeurs.

IPA [dᵊmãd s‿il a de fʁɛʁ e sœʁ || — wi | i l‿a œ̃ fʁɛʁ e dø sœʁ ||]

502

EN I don't have a computer.

FR Je n'ai pas d'ordinateur.

IPA [ʒø n‿ɛ pa d‿ɔʁdinatœʁ ||]

503

EN You don't have a dog.

FR Tu n'as pas de chien.

IPA [ty n‿a pa dø ʃjɛ̃ ||]

504

EN She doesn't have a bike.

FR Elle n'a pas de vélo.

IPA [ɛl n‿a pa dø velo ||]

505

EN He has several brothers and sisters.

FR Il a plusieurs frères et sœurs.
IPA [i l̯a plyzjœʁ fʁɛʁ e sœʁ ‖]

506

EN They have two (2) children.

FR Ils ont deux enfants.
IPA [i l̯ɔ̃ dø z̯ãfã ‖]

507

EN She doesn't have a key.

FR Elle n'a pas de clé.
IPA [ɛl n̯a pa dø kle ‖]

508

EN He has a new job.

FR Il a un nouveau travail.
IPA [i l̯a œ̃ nuvo tʁavaj ‖]

509

EN They don't have much money.

FR Ils (♀ elles) n'ont pas beaucoup d'argent.
IPA [il (♀ ɛl) n̯ɔ̃ pa boku d̯aʁʒã ‖]

510

EN Do you have an umbrella?

FR As-tu un parapluie?
IPA [a ty œ̃ paʁaplɥi ‖]

511

EN We have a lot of work to do.

FR Nous avons beaucoup de travail à faire. > On a beaucoup de travail à faire.
IPA [nu z‿avɔ̃ boku dø tʁavaj a fɛʁ ‖ > ɔ̃ n‿a boku dø tʁavaj a fɛʁ ‖]

512

EN I don't have your phone number.

FR Je n'ai pas ton numéro de téléphone.
IPA [ʒø n‿ɛ pa tɔ̃ nymeʁo dø telefɔn ‖]

513

EN Does your father have a car?

FR Ton père a-t-il une voiture?
IPA [tɔ̃ pɛʁ a t‿il yn vwatyʁ ‖]

514

EN How much money do you have with you?

FR Combien d'argent as-tu sur toi?
IPA [kɔ̃bjɛ̃ d‿aʁʒɑ̃ a ty syʁ twa ‖]

515

EN She doesn't have a car. She goes everywhere by bicycle.

FR Elle n'a pas de voiture. Elle se rend partout à vélo.
IPA [ɛl n‿a pa dø vwatyʁ || ɛl sø ʁ ̃a paʁtu a velo ||]

516

EN They like animals. They have three (3) dogs and two (2) cats.

FR Ils (♀ elles) aiment les animaux. Ils (♀ elles) ont trois chiens et deux chats.
IPA [il (♀ ɛl) ɛm le z‿animo || il (♀ ɛl) ɔ̃ tʁwa ʃjɛ̃ e dø ʃa ||]

517

EN Fahim isn't happy. He's got a lot of problems.

FR Fahim n'est pas heureux. Il a beaucoup de problèmes.
IPA [(...) n‿e pa z‿øʁø || i l‿a boku dø pʁoblɛm ||]

518

EN They don't read much. They don't have many books.

FR Ils (♀ elles) ne lisent pas beaucoup. Ils (♀ elles) n'ont pas beaucoup de livres.
IPA [il (♀ ɛl) nø liz pa boku || il (♀ ɛl) n‿ɔ̃ pa boku dø livʁ ||]

519

EN What's wrong? — I've got something in my eye.

FR Qu'est-ce qui ne va pas? — J'ai quelque chose dans l'œil.

IPA [kɛsᵒ ki nø va pa || — ʒ‿ɛ kɛlk ʃoz dɑ̃ l‿œj ||]

520

EN Where's my phone? — I don't know. I don't have it.

FR Où est mon téléphone? — Je ne sais pas. Je ne l'ai pas.

IPA [u e mɔ̃ telefɔn || — ʒø nø sɛ pa || ʒø nø l‿ɛ pa ||]

521

EN She wants to go to the concert, but she doesn't have a ticket.

FR Elle veut aller au concert, mais elle n'a pas de billet.

IPA [ɛl vø ale o kɔ̃sɛʁ | me ɛl n‿a pa dø bijɛ ||]

522

EN I'm not feeling well. I have a headache.

FR Je ne me sens pas bien. J'ai mal à la tête.

IPA [ʒø nø mø sɑ̃s pa bjɛ̃ || ʒ‿ɛ mal a la tɛt ||]

523

EN It's a nice house but it doesn't have a big yard.

FR C'est une belle maison, mais elle n'a pas de grand jardin.

IPA [sɛ t‿yn bɛl mɛzɔ̃ | mɛ ɛl n‿a pa dø gʁɑ̃ ʒaʁdɛ̃ ‖]

524

EN Most cars have four (4) wheels.

FR La plupart des voitures ont quatre roues.

IPA [la plypaʁ de vwatyʁ ɔ̃ katʁ ʁu ‖]

525

EN Everybody likes him. He's got a lot of friends.

FR Tout le monde l'aime. Il a beaucoup d'amis.

IPA [tu lø mɔ̃d l‿em ‖ i l‿a boku d‿ami ‖]

526

EN I can't open the door. I don't have the key.

FR Je ne peux pas ouvrir la porte. Je n'ai pas de clé.

IPA [ʒø nø pø pa z‿uvʁiʁ la pɔʁt ‖ ʒø n‿ɛ pa dø kle ‖]

527

EN An insect has six (6) legs.

FR Un insecte a six pattes.

IPA [œ̃ n‿ɛ̃sɛkt a sis pat ‖]

528

EN Hurry, we don't have much time.

FR Dépêche-toi, nous n'avons pas beaucoup de temps.
IPA [depɛʃ twa | nu n‿avɔ̃ pa boku dø tɑ̃ ‖]

529

EN Now he's at work.

FR Il est actuellement au travail.
IPA [i l‿e aktɥɛl³mɑ̃ o tʁavaj ‖]

530

EN Last night he wasn't at work.

FR Il n'était pas au travail hier soir.
IPA [il n‿etɛ pa o tʁavaj jɛʁ swaʁ ‖]

531

EN He was in bed.

FR Il était au lit.
IPA [i l‿etɛ o li ‖]

532

EN He was asleep.

FR Il dormait.
IPA [il dɔʁmɛ ‖]

533

EN He was in bed, asleep.

FR Il était au lit, endormi.
IPA [i l‿etɛ o li | ãdɔʁmi ‖]

534

EN I was tired last night.

FR J'étais fatigué (♀ fatiguée) hier soir.
IPA [ʒ‿etɛ fatige (♀ fatige) jɛʁ swaʁ ‖]

535

EN Where was Fatima yesterday?

FR Où était Fatima hier?
IPA [u etɛ (...) jɛʁ ‖]

536

EN The weather was nice last week.

FR Il faisait beau la semaine dernière.
IPA [il fᵊzɛ bo la sᵊmɛn dɛʁnjɛʁ ‖]

537

EN You were late yesterday.

FR Tu étais en retard hier.
IPA [ty etɛ z‿ã ʁᵊtaʁ jɛʁ ‖]

538

EN They weren't here last Sunday.

FR Ils (♀elles) n'étaient pas ici dimanche passé.
IPA [il (♀εl) n̩ete pa z̩isi dimɑ̃ʃ pase ‖]

539

EN Last year Rebecca was twenty-two (22), so she is twenty-three (23) now.

FR L'an dernier, Rebecca avait vingt-deux ans, alors elle en a maintenant vingt-trois.
IPA [l̩ɑ̃ dɛʁnje | (...) ave vɛ̃tdø z̩ɑ̃ | alɔ ʁ̩ε l̩ɑ̃ n̩a mɛ̃tᵊnɑ̃ vɛ̃ttʁwa ‖]

540

EN When I was a child, I was afraid of dogs.

FR Lorsque j'étais un enfant, j'avais peur des chiens.
IPA [lɔʁskᵊ ʒ̩etε œ̃ n̩ɑ̃fɑ̃ | ʒ̩ave pøʁ de ʃjɛ̃ ‖]

541

EN We were hungry after the trip, but we weren't tired.

FR Nous avions faim après le voyage, mais nous n'étions pas fatigués.
IPA [nu z̩avjɔ̃ fɛ̃ apʁε lø vwajaʒ | mε nu n̩etjɔ̃ pa fatige ‖]

542

EN The hotel was comfortable, but it wasn't expensive.

FR L'hôtel était confortable, mais il ne coûtait pas cher.
IPA [l̩ otɛl ete kɔ̃fɔʁtabl | mɛ il nø kute pa ʃɛʁ ‖]

543

EN Was the weather nice when you were on vacation?

FR Faisait-il beau lorsque tu étais en vacances?
IPA [fᵊzɛ t̬il bo lɔʁskᵊ ty ete z̬ɑ̃ vakɑ̃s ‖]

544

EN Your shoes are nice. Were they expensive?

FR Tes chaussures sont jolies. Ont-elles coûté cher?
IPA [te ʃosyʁ sɔ̃ ʒoli ‖ ɔ̃ t̬el kute ʃɛʁ ‖]

545

EN Why were you late this morning?

FR Pourquoi étais-tu en retard ce matin?
IPA [puʁkwa ete ty ɑ̃ ʁᵊtaʁ sø matɛ̃ ‖]

546

EN Were you late? — No, I wasn't.

FR Étais-tu en retard? — Non, je ne l'étais pas.
IPA [ete ty ɑ̃ ʁᵊtaʁ ‖ — nɔ̃ | ʒø nø l̩ete pa ‖]

547

EN Was Paul at work yesterday? — Yes, he was.

FR Paul était-il au travail hier? — Oui, il y était.
IPA [(...) ete t il o tʁavaj jɛʁ || — wi | i l i ete ||]

548

EN Were they at the party? — No, they weren't.

FR Étaient-ils (♀elles) à la fête? — Non, ils (♀elles) n'y étaient pas.
IPA [etɛ t il (♀ɛl) a la fɛt || — nɔ̃ | il (♀ɛl) n i ete pa ||]

549

EN Today the weather's nice, but yesterday it was very cold.

FR Le temps est beau aujourd'hui, mais il faisait très froid hier.
IPA [lø tɑ̃ e bo oʒuʁdɥi | mɛ il fᵊzɛ tʁɛ fʁwa jɛʁ ||]

550

EN I'm hungry. Can I have something to eat?

FR J'ai faim. Puis-je avoir quelque chose à manger?
IPA [ʒ ɛ fɛ̃ || pɥi ʒø avwaʁ kɛlk ʃoz a mɑ̃ʒe ||]

551

EN I feel fine this morning, but I was very tired last night.

FR Je me sens bien ce matin, mais j'étais très fatigué (♀ fatiguée) hier soir.

IPA [ʒø mø sɑ̃s bjɛ̃ sø matɛ̃ | mɛ ʒ‿ete tʁɛ fatige (♀ fatige) jeʁ swaʁ ‖]

552

EN Where were you at eleven a.m. (11:00) last Friday morning?

FR Où étais-tu à onze heures vendredi dernier?

IPA [u etɛ ty a ɔ̃z œʁ vɑ̃dʁᵊdi dɛʁnje ‖]

553

EN Don't buy those shoes. They're very expensive.

FR N'achète pas ces chaussures. Elles coûtent très cher.

IPA [n‿aʃɛt pa se ʃosyʁ ‖ ɛl kut tʁɛ ʃeʁ ‖]

554

EN I like your new jacket. Was it expensive?

FR J'aime ton nouveau veston. A-t-il coûté cher?

IPA [ʒ‿ɛm tɔ̃ nuvo vɛstɔ̃ ‖ a t‿il kute ʃeʁ ‖]

555

EN This time last year I was in Paris.

FR À cette date, l'an dernier, j'étais à Paris.
IPA [a sɛt dat | lɑ̃ dɛʁnje | ʒ‿ete a (...) ||]

556

EN Where are the children? — I don't know, they were here a few minutes ago.

FR Où sont les enfants? — Je ne sais pas, ils (♀ elles) étaient là il y a quelques minutes.
IPA [u sɔ̃ le z‿ɑ̃fɑ̃ || — ʒø nø sɛ pa | il (♀ ɛl) ete la i l‿i a kɛlk minyt ||]

557

EN We weren't happy with the hotel. Our room was very small, and it wasn't clean.

FR Nous n'étions pas satisfaits de l'hôtel. Notre chambre était petite et elle n'était pas propre.
IPA [nu n‿etjɔ̃ pa satisfɛ dø l‿otɛl || nɔtʁ ʃɑ̃bʁ ete pᵊtit e ɛl n‿ete pa pʁɔpʁ ||]

558

EN Antonio wasn't at work last week because he was sick. He's better now.

FR Antonio n'était pas au travail la semaine dernière parce qu'il était malade. Il va mieux maintenant.
IPA [(...) n‿ete pa o tʁavaj la sᵊmɛn dɛʁnjɛʁ paʁs k‿il ete malad || il va mjø mɛ̃tᵊnɑ̃ ||]

559

EN Yesterday was a holiday, so the banks were closed. They're open today.

FR Hier était un jour férié, alors les banques étaient fermées. Elles sont ouvertes aujourd'hui.

IPA [jɛ ʁ‿ete t‿œ̃ ʒuʁ feʁje | alɔʁ le bɑ̃k ete feʁme || ɛl sɔ̃ uvɛʁt oʒuʁdɥi ||]

560

EN Were Anabel and Richard at the party? — Anabel was there, but Richard wasn't.

FR Est-ce qu'Anabel et Richard étaient à la fête? — Anabel y était, mais pas Richard.

IPA [ɛs° k (...) e (...) ete a la fɛt || — (...) i ete | mɛ pa (...) ||]

561

EN Where are my keys? — I don't know. They were on the table, but they're not there now.

FR Où sont mes clés? — Je ne sais pas. Elles étaient sur la table, mais elles n'y sont pas maintenant.

IPA [u sɔ̃ me kle || — ʒø nø sɛ pa || ɛ l‿ete syʁ la tabl | mɛ ɛl n‿i sɔ̃ pa mɛ̃t°nɑ̃ ||]

562

EN You weren't at home last night. Where were you?

FR Tu n'étais pas à la maison hier soir. Où étais-tu?

IPA [ty n‿etɛ pa a la mɛzɔ̃ jɛʁ swaʁ || u etɛ ty ||]

563

EN Why were you late this morning? — The traffic was bad.

FR Pourquoi étais-tu en retard ce matin? — La circulation était mauvaise.

IPA [puʁkwa etɛ ty ɑ̃ ʁ°taʁ sø matɛ̃ || — la siʁkylasjɔ̃ etɛ movɛz ||]

564

EN Was your exam difficult? — No, it was easy.

FR Est-ce que ton examen était difficile? — Non, il était facile.

IPA [ɛs° kø tɔ̃ n‿ɛgzamɛ̃ etɛ difisil || — nɔ̃ | i l‿etɛ fasil ||]

565

EN Where were they last week? — They were on vacation.

FR Où étaient-ils (♀elles) la semaine dernière? — Ils (♀elles) étaient en vacances.

IPA [u etɛ t‿il (♀ɛl) la s°mɛn dɛʁnjɛʁ || — il (♀ɛl) etɛ t‿ɑ̃ vakɑ̃s ||]

566

EN How much was your new camera? — It was three hundred dollars ($300). > It was two hundred euros (€200).

FR Combien était ta nouvelle caméra? — Elle était deux cents euros.

IPA [kɔ̃bjɛ̃ n‿ete ta nuvɛl kameʁa ‖ — ɛ l‿ete dø sɑ̃ z‿øʁo ‖]

567

EN Why were you angry yesterday? — Because you were late.

FR Pourquoi étais-tu fâché (♀ fâchée) hier? — Parce que tu étais en retard.

IPA [puʁkwa ete ty faʃe (♀ faʃe) jɛʁ ‖ — paʁs kø ty ete z‿ɑ̃ ʁ°taʁ ‖]

568

EN Was the weather nice last week? — Yes, it was beautiful.

FR Faisait-il beau la semaine dernière? — Oui, c'était magnifique.

IPA [f°zɛ t‿il bo la s°mɛn dɛʁnjɛʁ ‖ — wi | se ete maɲifik ‖]

569

EN   I brush my teeth every morning. This morning I brushed my teeth.

FR   Je me brosse les dents tous les matins. Ce matin, je me suis brossé les dents.

IPA   [ʒø mø bʁɔs le dɑ̃ tu le matɛ̃ || sø matɛ̃ | ʒø mø sɥi bʁose le dɑ̃ ||]

570

EN   Terry worked in a bank from nineteen ninety-five (1995) to two thousand one (2001).

FR   Terry a travaillé dans une banque de mille neuf cents quatre-vingt-quinze (1995) à deux mille un (2001).

IPA   [(...) a tʁavaje dɑ̃ z‿yn bɑ̃k dø mil nœf sɑ̃ katʁᵊvɛ̃kɛ̃z (1995) a dø mil ɛ̃̃ (2001) ||]

571

EN   Yesterday it rained all morning. It stopped at lunchtime.

FR   Hier, il a plu toute la matinée. La pluie a cessé à l'heure du déjeuner.

IPA   [jɛʁ | i l‿a ply tut la matine || la plɥi a sese a l‿œʁ dy deʒœne ||]

572

EN   We enjoyed the party last night.

FR   Nous avons aimé la fête hier soir.

IPA   [nu z‿avɔ̃ eme la fɛt jɛʁ swaʁ ||]

573

EN We danced a lot and talked to a lot of people.

FR Nous avons beaucoup dansé et nous avons parlé à beaucoup de gens. > On a beaucoup dansé et on a parlé à beaucoup de gens.

IPA [nu z̯avɔ̃ boku dɑ̃se e nu z̯avɔ̃ paʁle a boku dø ʒɑ̃ ‖ > ɔ̃ n̯a boku dɑ̃se e ɔ̃ n̯a paʁle a boku dø ʒɑ̃ ‖]

574

EN The party ended at midnight.

FR La fête a fini à minuit.

IPA [la fɛt a fini a minɥi ‖]

575

EN I usually get up early, but this morning I got up at nine thirty (9:30).

FR Je me lève généralement tôt, mais ce matin je me suis levé à neuf heures trente (9 h 30).

IPA [ʒø mø lɛv ʒeneʁalᵊmɑ̃ to | mɛ sø matɛ̃ ʒø mø sɥi lᵊve a nœ v̯œʁ tʁɑ̃t (9 h 30) ‖]

576

EN We did a lot of work yesterday.

FR Nous avons beaucoup travaillé hier. > On a beaucoup travaillé hier.

IPA [nu z̯avɔ̃ boku tʁavaje jɛʁ ‖ > ɔ̃ n̯a boku tʁavaje jɛʁ ‖]

577

EN Sonia went to the movies three (3) times last week.

FR Sonia est allée au cinéma trois fois cette semaine.
IPA [(...) e t‿ale o sinema tʁwa fwa sɛt s°mɛn ‖]

578

EN Enzo came into the room, took off his coat, and sat down.

FR Enzo est entré dans la pièce, a enlevé son manteau et s'est assis.
IPA [(...) e ɑ̃tʁe dɑ̃ la pjɛs | a ɑ̃l°ve sɔ̃ mɑ̃to e s‿e asi ‖]

579

EN It was hot in the room, so I opened the window.

FR Il faisait chaud dans la pièce, alors j'ai ouvert la fenêtre.
IPA [il f°zɛ ʃo dɑ̃ la pjɛs | alɔʁ ʒ‿e uvɛʁ la f°nɛtʁ ‖]

580

EN The movie was very long. It started at seven-fifteen (7:15) and finished at ten pm (10:00).

FR Le film était très long. Il a commencé à dix-neuf heures quinze (19 h 15) et a fini à vingt-deux heures (22 h).
IPA [lø film etɛ tʁɛ lɔ̃ ‖ i l‿a komɑ̃se a diznœ v‿œʁ kɛ̃z (19 h 15) e a fini a vɛ̃tdø z‿œʁ (22 h) ‖]

581

EN When I was a child, I wanted to be a doctor.

FR Lorsque j'étais un enfant, je voulais devenir médecin.

IPA [lɔʁskə ʒ‿ete œ̃ n‿ɑ̃fɑ̃ | ʒø vule dᵊvᵊniʁ mɛdsɛ̃ ‖]

582

EN The accident happened last Sunday afternoon.

FR L'accident est survenu dimanche dernier en après-midi.

IPA [l‿aksidɑ̃ e syʁvᵊny dimɑ̃ʃ dɛʁnje ɑ̃ apʁɛ midi ‖]

583

EN It's a nice day today, but yesterday it rained all day.

FR C'est une belle journée aujourd'hui, mais il a plu toute la journée hier.

IPA [sɛ t‿yn bɛl ʒuʁne oʒuʁdɥi | mɛ i l‿a ply tut la ʒuʁne jɛʁ ‖]

584

EN We enjoyed our vacation last year. We stayed at a very nice place.

FR Nous avons aimé nos vacances l'an dernier. Nous avons séjourné à un très bel endroit.

IPA [nu z‿avɔ̃ eme no vakɑ̃s l‿ɑ̃ dɛʁnje ‖ nu z‿avɔ̃ seʒuʁne a œ̃ tʁɛ bɛ l‿ɑ̃dʁwa ‖]

585

EN Cecilia's grandfather died when he was ninety (90)
     years old.

FR Le grand-père de Cecilia est mort à quatre-vingt-dix
     ans.
IPA [lø gʁɑ̃pɛʁ dø (...) e mɔʁ a katʁ°vẽdi z̥ã ||]

586

EN I already paid the bill.

FR J'ai déjà payé la note.
IPA [ʒ̊ɛ deʒa peje la nɔt ||]

587

EN I visited her last week.

FR Je l'ai visitée la semaine dernière.
IPA [ʒø l̥ɛ vizite la s°mɛn dɛʁnjɛʁ ||]

588

EN I bought my tickets online.

FR J'ai acheté mes billets en ligne.
IPA [ʒ̊ɛ aʃ°te me bijɛ ã liɲ ||]

589

EN I copied the schedule.

FR J'ai copié l'horaire.
IPA [ʒ̊ɛ kopje l̥ɔʁɛʁ ||]

590

EN I put my bag on the table. (PAST TENSE)

FR J'ai mis mon sac sur la table.
IPA [ʒ‿ɛ mi mɔ̃ sak syʁ la tabl ‖]

591

EN I spoke with him yesterday on the phone.

FR J'ai discuté avec lui hier au téléphone.
IPA [ʒ‿ɛ diskyte avɛk lɥi jɛʁ o telefɔn ‖]

592

EN Last Tuesday, Vanessa flew from Los Angeles to Mexico City.

FR Mardi dernier, Vanessa a volé de Los Angeles à Mexico.
IPA [maʁdi dɛʁnje | (...) a vole dø (...) a mɛksiko ‖]

593

EN She got up at six (6) in the morning and had a cup of coffee.

FR Elle s'est levée à six heures et a bu une tasse de café.
IPA [ɛl s‿e lᵊve a si z‿œʁ e a by yn tas dø kafe ‖]

594

EN At seven-fifteen she left home and drove to the airport.

FR À sept heures quinze (7 h 15), elle a quitté la maison et a conduit jusqu'à l'aéroport.

IPA [a sɛ t‿œʁ kɛ̃z (7 h 15) | ɛ l‿a kite la mɛzɔ̃ e a kɔ̃dɥi ʒyska l‿aeʁopɔʁ ‖]

595

EN When she got there, she parked the car, walked to the terminal, and checked in.

FR Quand elle est arrivée là-bas, elle a garé sa voiture, a marché jusqu'au terminal et s'est enregistrée.

IPA [kɑ̃ d‿ɛ l‿e t‿aʁive laba | ɛ l‿a gaʁe sa vwatyʁ | a maʁʃe ʒysko tɛʁminal e s‿e ɑ̃ʁ°ʒistʁe ‖]

596

EN Then she had breakfast at an airport cafe and waited for her flight.

FR Ensuite, elle a pris le petit déjeuner dans un café de l'aéroport et a attendu son vol.

IPA [ɑ̃sɥit | ɛ l‿a pʁi lø p°ti deʒœne dɑ̃ z‿œ̃ kafe dø l‿aeʁopɔʁ e a atɑ̃dy sɔ̃ vɔl ‖]

597

EN The plane departed on time and arrived in Mexico City four (4) hours later.

FR L'avion a décollé à l'heure et est arrivé à Mexico quatre heures plus tard.

IPA [l̪avjɔ̃ a dekole a l̪ œʁ e e t̪aʁive a mɛksiko katʁ œʁ plys taʁ ‖]

598

EN Finally, she took a taxi from the airport to her hotel downtown.

FR Finalement, elle a pris un taxi de l'aéroport jusqu'à son hôtel, au centre-ville.

IPA [final°mɑ̃ | ɛ l̪a pʁi z̪œ taksi dø l̪aeʁopɔʁ ʒyska sɔ̃ n̪otɛl | o sɑ̃tʁ°vil ‖]

599

EN Steve always goes to work by car. > Yesterday he went to work by car.

FR Steve se rend toujours au travail en voiture. Hier, il est allé au travail en voiture.

IPA [(...) sø ʁɑ̃ tuʒuʁ o tʁavaj ɑ̃ vwatyʁ ‖ jɛʁ | i l̪e ale o tʁavaj ɑ̃ vwatyʁ ‖]

600

EN Hannah often loses her keys. > She lost her keys last week.

FR Hannah perd souvent ses clés. Elle a perdu ses clés la semaine dernière.

IPA [(...) pɛʁ suvã se kle || ɛ l̪a pɛʁdy se kle la s°mɛn dɛʁnjɛʁ ||]

GMS #601 - 700

601

EN Zoe meets her friends every night. > She met them last night.

FR Zoë voit ses amis (♀amies) tous les soirs. Elle les a vus (♀vues) hier soir.

IPA [(...) vwa se z‿ami (♀ami) tu le swaʁ || ɛl le z‿a vy (♀vy) jɛʁ swaʁ ||]

602

EN I usually buy two (2) newspapers every day. > Yesterday I bought two (2) newspapers.

FR J'achète généralement deux journaux tous les jours. Hier, j'ai acheté deux journaux.

IPA [ʒ‿aʃɛt ʒeneʁal°mã dø ʒuʁno tu le ʒuʁ || jɛʁ | ʒ‿ɛ aʃ°te dø ʒuʁno ||]

603

EN We often go to the movies on weekends. > Last Sunday we went to the movies.

FR Nous allons souvent au cinéma les week-ends. Dimanche dernier, nous sommes allés (♀allées) au cinéma.

IPA [nu z‿alɔ̃ suvã o sinema le wikɛnd || dimãʃ dɛʁnje | nu sɔm ale (♀ale) o sinema ||]

604

EN I eat an orange every day. > Yesterday I ate an orange.

FR Je mange une orange tous les jours. Hier, j'ai mangé une orange.

IPA [ʒø mɑ̃ʒ yn oʁɑ̃ʒ tu le ʒuʁ || jɛʁ | ʒ‿ɛ mɑ̃ʒe yn oʁɑ̃ʒ ||]

605

EN Tom always takes a shower in the morning. > This morning he took a shower.

FR Tom se douche toujours le matin. Ce matin, il a pris une douche.

IPA [(...) sø duʃ tuʒuʁ lø matɛ̃ || sø matɛ̃ | i l‿a pʁi z‿yn duʃ ||]

606

EN Our friends often come to see us. > They came to see us last Friday.

FR Nos amis (♀amies) viennent souvent nous voir. Ils (♀elles) sont venus (♀venues) nous voir vendredi dernier.

IPA [no z‿ami (♀ami) vjɛn suvɑ̃ nu vwaʁ || il (♀ɛl) sɔ̃ v°ny (♀v°ny) nu vwaʁ vɑ̃dʁ°di dɛʁnje ||]

607

EN I don't watch TV very often.

FR Je ne regarde pas la télé très souvent.
IPA [ʒø nø ʁ°gaʁd pa la tele tʁɛ suvã ‖]

608

EN I didn't watch TV yesterday.

FR Je n'ai pas regardé la télé hier.
IPA [ʒø n‿ɛ pa ʁ°gaʁde la tele jɛʁ ‖]

609

EN Does she go out often?

FR Est-ce qu'elle sort souvent?
IPA [ɛs° k‿ɛl sɔʁ suvã ‖]

610

EN Did she go out last night?

FR Est-ce qu'elle est sortie hier soir?
IPA [ɛs° k‿ɛl e sɔʁti jɛʁ swaʁ ‖]

611

EN I played tennis yesterday, but I didn't win.

FR J'ai joué au tennis hier, mais je n'ai pas gagné.
IPA [ʒ‿ɛ ʒwe o tenis jɛʁ | mɛ ʒø n‿ɛ pa gaɲe ‖]

612

EN Did you do your homework? — No, I didn't have time.

FR As-tu fait tes devoirs? — Non, je n'ai pas eu le temps.

IPA [a ty fɛ te dᵊvwaʁ ‖ — nɔ̃ | ʒø n‿ɛ pa z‿y lø tɑ̃ ‖]

613

EN We went to the movies, but we didn't enjoy the film.

FR Nous sommes allés (♀allées) au cinéma, mais nous n'avons pas aimé le film.

IPA [nu sɔm ale (♀ale) o sinema | mɛ nu n‿avɔ̃ pa z‿eme lø film ‖]

614

EN Did you see Fabian yesterday? — No, I didn't.

FR As-tu vu Fabian hier? — Non, je ne l'ai pas vu.

IPA [a ty vy (...) jɛʁ ‖ — nɔ̃ | ʒø nø l‿ɛ pa vy ‖]

615

EN Did it rain on Sunday? — Yes, it did.

FR A-t-il plu dimanche? — Oui, il a plu.

IPA [a t‿il ply dimɑ̃ʃ ‖ — wi | i l‿a ply ‖]

616

EN Did Eveline come to the party? — No, she didn't.

FR Est-ce qu'Eveline est venue à la fête? — Non, elle n'est pas venue.

IPA [ɛsº k (...) e vºny a la fɛt ǁ — nɔ̃ | ɛl n̩e pa vºny ǁ]

617

EN Did your parents have a good trip? — Yes, they did.

FR Est-ce que tes parents ont fait un beau voyage? — Oui, ils ont fait un beau voyage.

IPA [ɛsº kø te paʁɑ̃ ɔ̃ fɛ t̩œ̃ bo vwajaʒ ǁ — wi | i l̩ɔ̃ fɛ t̩œ̃ bo vwajaʒ ǁ]

618

EN I saw Evita, but I didn't see Fausto.

FR J'ai vu Evita, mais je n'ai pas vu Fausto.

IPA [ʒ̩ɛ vy (...) | mɛ ʒø n̩ɛ pa vy (...) ǁ]

619

EN They worked on Monday, but they didn't on Tuesday.

FR Ils (♀elles) ont travaillé lundi, mais pas mardi.

IPA [il (♀ɛl) ɔ̃ tʁavaje lœ̃di | mɛ pa maʁdi ǁ]

620

EN We went to the post office, but we didn't go to the bank.

FR Nous sommes allés (♀allées) au bureau de poste, mais nous ne sommes pas allés (♀allées) à la banque.

IPA [nu sɔm ale (♀ale) o byʁo də pɔst | mɛ nu nø sɔm pa z‿ale (♀ale) a la bɑ̃k ‖]

621

EN She had a pen, but she didn't have any paper.

FR Elle avait un stylo, mais elle n'avait pas de papier.

IPA [ɛ l‿avɛ t‿œ̃ stilo | mɛ ɛl n‿avɛ pa də papje ‖]

622

EN Gerhard did some work in the yard, but he didn't do any work in the house.

FR Gerhard a travaillé un peu dans le jardin, mais n'a pas travaillé dans la maison.

IPA [(...) a tʁavaje œ̃ pø dɑ̃ lø ʒaʁdɛ̃ | mɛ n‿a pa tʁavaje dɑ̃ la mɛzɔ̃ ‖]

623

EN I watched TV last night. How about you? Did you watch TV last night?

FR J'ai regardé la télé hier soir. Et toi? As-tu regardé la télé hier soir?

IPA [ʒ‿ɛ ʁᵊgaʁde la tele jɛʁ swaʁ || e twa || a ty ʁᵊgaʁde la tele jɛʁ swaʁ ||]

624

EN I enjoyed the party. How about you? Did you enjoy the party?

FR J'ai aimé la fête. Et toi? As-tu aimé la fête?

IPA [ʒ‿ɛ eme la fɛt || e twa || a ty eme la fɛt ||]

625

EN I had a nice vacation. How about you? Did you have a nice vacation?

FR J'ai eu de belles vacances. Et toi? As-tu eu de belles vacances?

IPA [ʒ‿ɛ y dø bɛl vakãs || e twa || a ty y dø bɛl vakãs ||]

626

EN I finished work early. How about you? Did you finish work early?

FR J'ai fini mon travail plus tôt. Et toi? As-tu fini ton travail plus tôt?

IPA [ʒ‿ɛ fini mɔ̃ tʁavaj plys to || e twa || a ty fini tɔ̃ tʁavaj plys to ||]

627

EN I slept well last night. How about you? Did you sleep well last night?

FR J'ai bien dormi hier soir. Et toi? As-tu bien dormi hier soir?

IPA [ʒ‿ɛ bjɛ̃ dɔʁmi jɛʁ swaʁ ‖ e twa ‖ a ty bjɛ̃ dɔʁmi jɛʁ swaʁ ‖|]

628

EN I watched TV.

FR J'ai regardé la télé.

IPA [ʒ‿ɛ ʁᵊgaʁde la tele ‖|]

629

EN I got up before seven am (7:00).

FR Je me suis levé avant sept heures (7 h).

IPA [ʒø mø sɥi lᵊve avɑ̃ sɛ t‿œʁ (7 h) ‖|]

630

EN I took a shower.

FR J'ai pris une douche.

IPA [ʒ‿ɛ pʁi z‿yn duʃ ‖|]

631

EN I bought a magazine.

FR J'ai acheté un magazine.
IPA [ʒ‿ɛ aʃ°te œ̃ magazin ‖]

632

EN I went to bed before ten-thirty.

FR Je suis allé au lit avant vingt-deux heures trente (22 h 30).
IPA [ʒø sɥi ale o li avɑ̃ vɛ̃tdø z‿œʁ tʁɑ̃t (22 h 30) ‖]

633

EN We went to Hong Kong last month.

FR Nous sommes allés (♀ allées) à Hong Kong le mois dernier.
IPA [nu sɔm ale (♀ ale) a (...) lø mwa dɛʁnje ‖]

634

EN Where did you stay?

FR Où avez-vous séjourné?
IPA [u ave vu seʒuʁne ‖]

635

EN We stayed with some friends.

FR Nous avons séjourné chez des amis (♀ amies).
IPA [nu z‿avɔ̃ seʒuʁne ʃe de z‿ami (♀ ami) ‖]

636

EN I was late for the meeting.

FR J'étais en retard à la réunion.
IPA [ʒ‿etɛ ɑ̃ ʁ°taʁ a la ʁeynjɔ̃ ‖]

637

EN What time did you get there?

FR À quelle heure es-tu arrivé (♀ arrivée)?
IPA [a kɛ l‿œʁ ɛ ty aʁive (♀ aʁive) ‖]

638

EN I got there at nine-thirty.

FR Je suis arrivé à neuf heures trente (9 h 30).
IPA [ʒø sɥi aʁive a nœ v‿œʁ tʁɑ̃t (9 h 30) ‖]

639

EN I played tennis this afternoon.

FR J'ai joué au tennis cet après-midi.
IPA [ʒ‿ɛ ʒwe o tenis sɛt apʁɛ midi ‖]

640

EN Did you win?

FR As-tu gagné?
IPA [a ty gaɲe ‖]

641

EN No, I lost.

FR Non, j'ai perdu.
IPA [nɔ̃ | ʒ‿ɛ pɛʁdy ‖]

642

EN I had a nice vacation.

FR J'ai eu de belles vacances.
IPA [ʒ‿ɛ y də bɛl vakɑ̃s ‖]

643

EN Where did you go?

FR Où es-tu allé (♀allée)?
IPA [u ɛ ty ale (♀ale) ‖]

644

EN I went to the mountains.

FR Je suis allé (♀allée) dans les montagnes.
IPA [ʒø sɥi ale (♀ale) dɑ̃ le mɔ̃taɲ ‖]

645

EN We came home by taxi.

FR Nous sommes rentrés (♀rentrées) en taxi.
IPA [nu sɔm ʁɑ̃tʁe (♀ʁɑ̃tʁe) ɑ̃ taksi ‖]

646

EN How much did it cost?

FR Combien ça a coûté?
IPA [kɔ̃bjɛ̃ sa a kute ||]

647

EN It cost forty dollars ($40). > It cost thirty euros (€30)

FR Ça a coûté trente euros.
IPA [sa a kute tʁɑ̃t øʁo ||]

648

EN I'm tired this morning.

FR Je suis fatigué (♀ fatiguée) ce matin.
IPA [ʒø sɥi fatige (♀ fatige) sø matɛ̃ ||]

649

EN Did you sleep well last night?

FR As-tu bien dormi hier soir?
IPA [a ty bjɛ̃ dɔʁmi jɛʁ swaʁ ||]

650

EN No, I didn't sleep very well.

FR Non, je n'ai pas dormi très bien.
IPA [nɔ̃ | ʒø n‿ɛ pa dɔʁmi tʁɛ bjɛ̃ ||]

651

EN We went to the beach yesterday.

FR Nous sommes allés (♀ allées) à la plage hier. > On est allés (♀ allées) à la plage hier.

IPA [nu sɔm ale (♀ ale) a la plaʒ jɛʁ || > ɔ̃ n‿e ale (♀ ale) a la plaʒ jɛʁ ||]

652

EN Was the weather nice?

FR Est-ce qu'il faisait beau?

IPA [ɛsᵊ k‿il fᵊzɛ bo ||]

653

EN Yes, the weather was great.

FR Oui, il faisait super beau.

IPA [wi | il fᵊzɛ sypɛʁ bo ||]

654

EN The window is broken.

FR La fenêtre est cassée.

IPA [la fᵊnɛtʁ e kase ||]

655

EN How did it break?

FR Comment s'est-elle cassée?

IPA [komɑ̃ s‿e t‿ɛl kase ||]

656

EN I don't know how it broke.

FR Je ne sais pas comment elle s'est cassée.
IPA [ʒø nø sɛ pa kɔmɑ̃ t̪ɛl s̪e kase ‖]

657

EN We went to the movies, but the film wasn't very good. We didn't enjoy it.

FR Nous sommes allés (♀allées) au cinéma, mais le film n'était pas très bon. Nous ne l'avons pas aimé.
IPA [nu sɔm ale (♀ale) o sinema ǀ mɛ lø film n̪etɛ pa tʁɛ bɔ̃ ‖ nu nø l̪avɔ̃ pa z̪eme ‖]

658

EN Giovanni bought some new clothes yesterday: two (2) shirts and a pair of pants.

FR Giovanni a acheté de nouveaux vêtements hier : deux chemises et un pantalon.
IPA [(...) a aʃ°te dø nuvo vɛt°mɑ̃ jɛʁ ǀ dø ʃ°miz e œ̃ pɑ̃talɔ̃ ‖]

659

EN Did it rain yesterday? — No, it was a nice day.

FR A-t-il plu hier? — Non, il a fait beau.
IPA [a t̪il ply jɛʁ ‖ — nɔ̃ ǀ i l̪a fɛ bo ‖]

660

EN We were tired, so we didn't stay long at the party.

FR Nous étions fatigué (♀ fatiguées), alors nous ne sommes pas restés (♀ restées) à la fête très longtemps.

IPA [nu z‿etjɔ̃ fatige (♀ fatige) | alɔʁ nu nø sɔm pa ʁeste (♀ ʁeste) a la fɛt tʁɛ lɔ̃tɑ̃ ‖]

661

EN It was very warm in the room, so I opened a window.

FR Il faisait très chaud dans la pièce, alors j'ai ouvert une fenêtre.

IPA [il fᵊzɛ tʁɛ ʃo dɑ̃ la pjɛs | alɔʁ ʒ‿ɛ uvɛʁ ʁ‿yn fᵊnetʁ ‖]

662

EN Did you call Ingrid this morning? — No, I didn't have time.

FR As-tu appelé Ingrid ce matin? — Non, je n'ai pas eu le temps.

IPA [a ty apᵊle (...) sø matɛ̃ ‖ — nɔ̃ | ʒø n‿ɛ pa z‿y lø tɑ̃ ‖]

663

EN I cut my hand this morning. — How did you do that?

FR Je me suis coupé à la main ce matin. — Comment as-tu fait ça?

IPA [ʒø mø sɥi kupe a la mɛ̃ sø matɛ̃ ‖ — komɑ̃ a ty fɛ sa ‖]

664

EN Why weren't you at the meeting yesterday? — I
didn't know about a meeting.

FR Pourquoi n'étais-tu pas à la réunion hier? — Je n'étais
pas au courant de la réunion.

IPA [puʁkwa n̩ete ty pa a la ʁeynjɔ̃ jɛʁ ‖ — ʒø n̩ete pa
o kuʁɑ̃ dø la ʁeynjɔ̃ ‖]

665

EN It's six o'clock (6:00) now. Luka's at home watching
TV.

FR Il est actuellement dix-huit heures (18 h). Luka est à
la maison, en train de regarder la télé.

IPA [i l̩e aktɥɛl°mɑ̃ dizɥi t̩œʁ (18 h) ‖ (...) e a la mɛzɔ̃ |
ɑ̃ tʁɛ̃ dø ʁ°gaʁde la tele ‖]

666

EN At four o'clock (4:00) he wasn't at home. He was at
the gym.

FR À seize heures (16 h), il n'était pas à la maison. Il
était au gym.

IPA [a sɛz œʁ (16 h) | il n̩ete pa a la mɛzɔ̃ ‖ i l̩ete o ʒim
‖]

667

EN He was swimming in the pool, not watching TV.

FR Il nageait dans la piscine, il ne regardait pas la télé.

IPA [il naʒɛ dɑ̃ la pisin | il nø ʁ°gaʁdɛ pa la tele ‖]

668

EN What were you doing at eleven-thirty yesterday?
Were you working?

FR Que faisais-tu à onze heures trente (11 h 30) hier?
Travaillais-tu?
IPA [kø fᵊzɛ ty a ɔ̃z œʁ tʁɑ̃t (11 h 30) jeʁ ‖ tʁavaje ty ‖]

669

EN What did he say? — I don't know, I wasn't listening.

FR Qu'a-t-il dit? — Je ne sais pas, je n'écoutais pas.
IPA [k‿a t‿il di ‖ — ʒø nø sɛ pa ‖ ʒø n‿ekutɛ pa ‖]

670

EN It was raining, so we didn't go out.

FR Il pleuvait, alors nous ne sommes pas sortis
(♀ sorties).
IPA [il pløvɛ ‖ alɔʁ nu nø sɔm pa sɔʁti (♀ sɔʁti) ‖]

671

EN In two-thousand-one we were living in Japan.

FR En deux mille un (2001), nous vivions au Japon.
IPA [ɑ̃ dø mil œ̃ (2001) ‖ nu vivjɔ̃ o ʒapɔ̃ ‖]

672

EN Today she's wearing a skirt, but yesterday she was wearing pants.

FR Aujourd'hui, elle porte une jupe, mais hier elle portait un pantalon.
IPA [oʒuʁdɥi | ɛl pɔʁt yn ʒyp | mɛ je ʁ‿ɛl pɔʁtɛ t‿œ̃ pɑ̃talɔ̃ ||]

673

EN I woke up early yesterday. It was a beautiful morning.

FR Je me suis réveillé tôt hier. C'était un matin magnifique.
IPA [ʒø mø sɥi ʁeveje to t‿jɛʁ || se ete œ̃ matɛ̃ maɲifik ||]

674

EN The sun was shining, and the birds were singing.

FR Le soleil brillait et les oiseaux chantaient.
IPA [lø solɛj bʁijɛ e le z‿wazo ʃɑ̃tɛ ||]

675

EN I was working at ten-thirty last night.

FR Je travaillais à dix heures trente (10 h 30) hier soir.
IPA [ʒø tʁavajɛ a di z‿œʁ tʁɑ̃t (10 h 30) jɛʁ swaʁ ||]

676

EN It wasn't raining when we went out.

FR Il ne pleuvait pas quand nous sommes sortis
(♀ sorties).
IPA [il nø pløvɛ pa kɑ̃ nu sɔm sɔʁti (♀ sɔʁti) ‖]

677

EN What were you doing at three [o'clock] (3:00)?

FR Que faisais-tu à quinze heures (15 h)?
IPA [kø fᵊzɛ ty a kɛ̃z œʁ (15 h) ‖]

678

EN Dmitry and Irina were at the supermarket buying
food.

FR Dmitry et Irina faisaient les courses au supermarché.
IPA [(...) e (...) fᵊzɛ le kuʁs o sypɛʁmaʁʃe ‖]

679

EN Santo was in his car driving.

FR Santo était dans sa voiture et conduisait.
IPA [(...) etɛ dɑ̃ sa vwatyʁ e kɔ̃dɥizɛ ‖]

680

EN Dennis was at the station waiting for a train.

FR Dennis était à la gare et attendait un train.
IPA [(...) etɛ a la gaʁ e atɑ̃dɛ t‿œ̃ tʁɛ̃ ‖]

681

EN The old couple were in the park taking a walk.

FR Le vieux couple faisait une promenade au parc.
IPA [lø vjø kupl fᵊzɛ t̪yn pʁɔmnad o paʁk ‖]

682

EN At eight forty-five (8:45) she was washing her car.

FR À huit heures quarante-cinq (8 h 45), elle lavait sa
voiture.
IPA [a ɥi t̪œʁ kaʁɑ̃tsɛ̃k (8 h 45) | ɛl lavɛ sa vwatyʁ ‖]

683

EN At ten forty-five (10:45) she was playing tennis.

FR À dix heures quarante-cinq (10 h 45), elle jouait au
tennis.
IPA [a di z̪œʁ kaʁɑ̃tsɛ̃k (10 h 45) | ɛl ʒwɛ o tenis ‖]

684

EN At eight o'clock (8:00) she was reading the news.

FR À huit heures (8 h), elle lisait les nouvelles.
IPA [a ɥi t̪œʁ (8 h) | ɛl lizɛ le nuvɛl ‖]

685

EN At twelve-ten she was cooking lunch.

FR À midi dix (12 h 10), elle préparait le déjeuner.
IPA [a midi dis (12 h 10) | ɛl pʁepaʁɛ lø deʒœne ‖]

686

EN   At seven-fifteen (7:15) she was having breakfast.

FR   À sept heures quinze (7 h 15), elle prenait le petit déjeuner.

IPA [a sɛ t‿œʁ kɛ̃z (7 h 15) | ɛl pʁɔnɛ lø pºti deʒœne ‖]

687

EN   At nine thirty (9:30) she was cleaning the kitchen.

FR   À neuf heures trente (9 h 30), elle nettoyait la cuisine.

IPA [a nœ v‿œʁ tʁɑ̃t (9 h 30) | ɛl netwajɛ la kɥizin ‖]

688

EN   Where were you living in nineteen ninety-nine (1999)?

FR   Où habitais-tu en mille neuf cent quatre-vingt-dix-neuf (1999)?

IPA [u abitɛ ty ɑ̃ mil nœf sɑ̃ katʁºvɛ̃diznœf (1999) ‖]

689

EN   What were you doing at two [o'clock] (2:00)?

FR   Que faisais-tu à quatorze heures (14 h)?

IPA [kø fºzɛ ty a katɔʁz œʁ (14 h) ‖]

690

EN Was it raining when you got up?

FR Pleuvait-il quand tu t'es levé (♀levée)?
IPA [pløvε t‿il kɑ̃ ty t‿ε lᵊve (♀lᵊve) ‖]

691

EN Why was she driving so fast?

FR Pourquoi conduisait-elle si vite?
IPA [puʁkwa kɔ̃dɥize t‿εl si vit ‖]

692

EN Why was he wearing a suit yesterday?

FR Pourquoi portait-il un complet hier?
IPA [puʁkwa pɔʁtε t‿il œ̃ kɔ̃plε jεʁ ‖]

693

EN He wasn't wearing a jacket.

FR Il ne portait pas de veston.
IPA [il nø pɔʁtε pa dø vεstɔ̃ ‖]

694

EN He was carrying a bag.

FR Il transportait un sac.
IPA [il tʁɑ̃spɔʁtε t‿œ̃ sak ‖]

695

EN He wasn't going to the dentist.

FR Il n'allait pas chez le dentiste.
IPA [il n‿alɛ pa ʃe lø dɑ̃tist ||]

696

EN He was eating ice cream.

FR Il mangeait de la glace.
IPA [il mɑ̃ʒɛ dø la glas ||]

697

EN He wasn't carrying an umbrella.

FR Il ne transportait pas de parapluie.
IPA [il nø tʁɑ̃spɔʁtɛ pa dø paʁaplɥi ||]

698

EN He wasn't going home.

FR Il ne rentrait pas à la maison.
IPA [il nø ʁɑ̃tʁɛ pa a la mɛzɔ̃ ||]

699

EN He was wearing a hat.

FR Il portait un chapeau.
IPA [il pɔʁtɛ t‿œ̃ ʃapo ||]

700

EN He wasn't riding a bicycle.

FR Il ne se promenait pas à vélo.
IPA [il nø sø pʁɔmᵊnɛ pa a velo ‖]

GMS #701 - 800

701

EN What was Jose doing when the phone rang?

FR Que faisait Jose quand le téléphone a sonné?
IPA [kø fᵊzɛ (...) kɑ̃ lø telefɔn a sone ||]

702

EN He was reading a book.

FR Il lisait un livre.
IPA [il lizɛ t‿œ̃ livʁ ||]

703

EN What did he do when the phone rang?

FR Qu'a-t-il fait lorsque le téléphone a sonné?
IPA [k‿a t‿il fɛ lɔʁskᵊ lø telefɔn a sone ||]

704

EN He stopped reading and answered the phone.

FR Il a cessé de lire et a répondu au téléphone.
IPA [i l‿a sese dø liʁ e a ʁepɔ̃dy o telefɔn ||]

705

EN What did you do yesterday morning?

FR Qu'as-tu fait hier matin?
IPA [k‿a ty fɛ jɛʁ matɛ̃ ‖]

706

EN What were you doing at ten thirty (10:30)?

FR Que faisais-tu à dix heures trente (10 h 30)?
IPA [kø fᵊzɛ ty a di z‿œʁ tʁɑ̃t (10 h 30) ‖]

707

EN We played tennis from ten (10:00) to eleven thirty (11:30).

FR Nous avons joué au tennis de dix heures (10 h) à onze heures trente (11 h 30).
IPA [nu z‿avɔ̃ ʒwe o tenis dø di z‿œʁ (10 h) a ɔ̃z œʁ tʁɑ̃t (11 h 30) ‖]

708

EN We were playing tennis.

FR Nous jouions au tennis.
IPA [nu ʒujɔ̃ o tenis ‖]

709

EN Did you watch the basketball game on TV last night?

FR As-tu regardé la partie de basketball à télé hier soir?

IPA [a ty ʁ°gaʁde la paʁti dø (...) a tele jɛʁ swaʁ ‖]

710

EN Were you watching TV when I called you?

FR Regardais-tu la télé quand je t'ai appelé (♀appelée)?

IPA [ʁ°gaʁdɛ ty la tele kɑ̃ ʒø t̯ɛ ap°le (♀ap°le) ‖]

711

EN It didn't rain while we were on vacation.

FR Il n'a pas plu pendant que nous étions en vacances.

IPA [il n̯a pa ply pɑ̃dɑ̃ kø nu z̯etjɔ̃ z̯ɑ̃ vakɑ̃s ‖]

712

EN It wasn't raining when I got up.

FR Il ne pleuvait pas quand je me suis levé.

IPA [il nø pløvɛ pa kɑ̃ ʒø mø sɥi l°ve ‖]

713

EN I started work at nine (9:00) and finished at four thirty (4:30). So at two thirty (2:30), I was in the middle of working.

FR J'ai commencé à travailler à neuf heures (9 h) et j'ai fini à seize heures trente (16 h 30). Donc, à quatorze heures trente (14 h 30), j'étais en train de travailler.

IPA [ʒ‿ɛ komɑ̃se a tʁavaje a nœ v‿œʁ (9 h) e ʒ‿ɛ fini a sɛz œʁ tʁɑ̃t (16 h 30) || dɔ̃k | a katɔʁz œʁ tʁɑ̃t (14 h 30) | ʒ‿ete ɑ̃ tʁɛ̃ dø tʁavaje ||]

714

EN It was raining when we went out.

FR Il pleuvait quand nous sommes sortis (♀ sorties).

IPA [il pløvɛ kɑ̃ nu sɔm sɔʁti (♀ sɔʁti) ||]

715

EN I saw them this morning. They were waiting at the bus stop.

FR Je les ai vus (♀ vues) ce matin. Ils (♀ elles) attendaient à l'arrêt d'autobus.

IPA [ʒø le z‿ɛ vy (♀ vy) sø matɛ̃ || il (♀ ɛl) atɑ̃dɛ a l‿aʁɛ d‿otobys ||]

716

EN She fell asleep while reading.

FR Elle s'est endormie en lisant.

IPA [ɛl s‿e ɑ̃dɔʁmi ɑ̃ lizɑ̃ ||]

717

EN Khalid broke his arm last week.

FR Khalid s'est cassé le bras la semaine dernière.
IPA [(...) s‿e kase lø bʁa la sᵊmɛn dɛʁnjɛʁ ‖]

718

EN It happened when he was painting his room.

FR C'est arrivé alors qu'il peignait sa chambre.
IPA [sɛ t‿aʁive alɔʁ k‿il pɛɲɛ sa ʃɑ̃bʁ ‖]

719

EN He fell off the ladder.

FR Il est tombé de l'échelle.
IPA [i l‿e tɔ̃be dø l‿eʃɛl ‖]

720

EN The train arrived at the station, and she got off.

FR Le train est arrivé à la gare et elle est descendue.
IPA [lø tʁɛ̃ e t‿aʁive a la gaʁ e ɛ l‿e desɑ̃dy ‖]

721

EN Two friends of hers were waiting to meet her.

FR Deux de ses amis (♀amies) l'attendaient pour la voir.
IPA [dø dø se z‿ami (♀ami) l‿atɑ̃dɛ puʁ la vwaʁ ‖]

722

EN Yesterday she was walking down the street when she met Albert.

FR Hier, elle marchait dans la rue lorsqu'elle a rencontré Albert.

IPA [jɛʁ | ɛl maʁʃɛ dɑ̃ la ʁy lɔʁsk ɛl a ʁɑ̃kɔ̃tʁe (...) ||]

723

EN He was going to the station to catch a train, and he was carrying a bag.

FR Il allait à la gare pour prendre un train et il transportait un sac.

IPA [i l‿alɛ a la gaʁ puʁ pʁɑ̃dʁ œ̃ tʁɛ̃ e il tʁɑ̃spɔʁtɛ t‿œ̃ sak ||]

724

EN They stopped to talk for a few minutes.

FR Ils (♀elles) ont arrêté pour parler quelques minutes.

IPA [il (♀ɛl) ɔ̃ aʁete puʁ paʁle kɛlk minyt ||]

725

EN Was Lara busy when you went to see her?

FR Est-ce que Lara était occupée quand tu es allé (♀allée) la voir?

IPA [ɛs° kø (...) etɛ okype kɑ̃ ty ɛ ale (♀ale) la vwaʁ ||]

726

EN Yes, she was studying.

FR Oui, elle étudiait.
IPA [wi | ɛ l̪etydjɛ ||]

727

EN What time did the mail arrive this morning?

FR À quelle heure le courrier est-il arrivé ce matin?
IPA [a kɛ l̪œʁ lø kuʁje e t̪il aʁive sø matɛ̃ ||]

728

EN It came while he was having breakfast.

FR Il est arrivé alors qu'il prenait le petit déjeuner.
IPA [i l̪e t̪aʁive alɔʁ k̪il pʁønɛ lø p°ti deʒœne ||]

729

EN Was Marta at work today?

FR Est-ce que Marta était au travail aujourd'hui?
IPA [ɛs° kø (...) etɛ o tʁavaj oʒuʁdɥi ||]

730

EN No, she didn't go to work. She was sick.

FR Non, elle n'est pas allée au travail, elle était malade.
IPA [nɔ̃ | ɛl n̪e pa z̪ale o tʁavaj | ɛ l̪etɛ malad ||]

731

EN How fast were you driving when the police stopped you?

FR À quelle vitesse conduisais-tu quand la police t'a arrêté (♀ arrêtée)?

IPA [a kɛl vitɛs kɔ̃dɥizɛ ty kɑ̃ la polis t‿a aʁete (♀ aʁete) ‖]

732

EN I'm not sure, but I wasn't driving very fast.

FR Je n'en suis pas certain (♀ certaine), mais je ne conduisais pas très vite.

IPA [ʒø n‿ɑ̃ sɥi pa sɛʁtɛ̃ (♀ sɛʁtɛn) | me ʒø nø kɔ̃dɥizɛ pa tʁɛ vit ‖]

733

EN Did your team win the baseball game yesterday?

FR Est-ce que ton équipe a gagné la partie de baseball hier?

IPA [ɛsᵊ kø tɔ̃ n‿ekip a gaɲe la paʁti dø bezbol jɛʁ ‖]

734

EN No, the weather was very bad, so we didn't play.

FR Non, il faisait très mauvais, alors nous n'avons pas joué.

IPA [nɔ̃ | il fᵊzɛ tʁɛ movɛ | alɔʁ nu n‿avɔ̃ pa ʒwe ‖]

735

EN We were playing baseball when I hit the ball and broke a window.

FR Nous jouions au baseball quand j'ai frappé la balle et cassé une vitre.

IPA [nu ʒujɔ̃ o bezbol kɑ̃ ʒ‿ɛ fʁape la bal e kase yn vitʁ ‖]

736

EN Did you see Clara last night?

FR As-tu vu Clara hier soir?

IPA [a ty vy (...) jɛʁ swaʁ ‖]

737

EN Yes, she was wearing a very nice jacket.

FR Oui, elle portait un très beau veston.

IPA [wi | ɛl pɔʁtɛ t‿œ̃ tʁɛ bo vɛstɔ̃ ‖]

738

EN What were you doing at two [o'clock] (2:00) this morning?

FR Que faisais-tu à deux heures (2 h) du matin?

IPA [kø fᵊzɛ ty a dø z‿œʁ (2 h) dy matɛ̃ ‖]

739

EN I was asleep.

FR Je dormais.
IPA [ʒø dɔʁmɛ ‖]

740

EN I lost my key last night.

FR J'ai perdu ma clé la nuit dernière.
IPA [ʒ‿ɛ pɛʁdy ma kle la nɥi dɛʁnjɛʁ ‖]

741

EN How did you get into your apartment?

FR Comment es-tu entré dans ton appartement?
IPA [komã ɛ ty ãtʁe dã tõ n‿apaʁt°mã ‖]

742

EN I climbed in through a window.

FR J'ai escaladé la fenêtre.
IPA [ʒ‿ɛ ɛskalade la f°nɛtʁ ‖]

743

EN Bernard used to work in a factory.

FR Bernard travaillait dans une usine.
IPA [(...) tʁavajɛ dã z‿yn yzin ‖]

744

EN Now he works in a supermarket.

FR Maintenant, il travaille dans un supermarché.

IPA [mɛ̃t°nɑ̃ | il tʁavaj dɑ̃ z‿œ̃ sypɛʁmaʁʃe ‖]

745

EN When I was a child, I used to like chocolate.

FR Quand j'étais un enfant, j'aimais le chocolat.

IPA [kɑ̃ ʒ‿etɛ œ̃ n‿ɑ̃fɑ̃ | ʒ‿emɛ lø ʃokola ‖]

746

EN I used to read a lot of books, but I don't read much these days.

FR J'avais l'habitude de lire beaucoup de livres, mais je ne lis plus beaucoup ces jours-ci.

IPA [ʒ‿avɛ l‿abityd dø liʁ boku dø livʁ | me ʒø nø lis plys boku se ʒuʁ si ‖]

747

EN Emilia has short hair now, but it used to be very long.

FR Emilia a les cheveux courts maintenant, mais avant, elle les avait très longs.

IPA [(...) a le ʃ°vø kuʁ mɛ̃t°nɑ̃ | me avɑ̃ | ɛl le z‿avɛ tʁɛ lɔ̃ ‖]

748

EN They used to live on the same street as us.

FR Ils (♀elles) habitaient sur la même rue que nous.
IPA [il (♀εl) abitε syʁ la mεm ʁy kø nu ‖]

749

EN We used to see them a lot, but we don't see them very often these days.

FR Nous avions l'habitude de les voir souvent, mais nous ne les voyons plus très souvent ces jours-ci.
IPA [nu z‿avjɔ̃ l‿abityd dø le vwaʁ suvɑ̃ | mε nu nø le vwajɔ̃ plys tʁε suvɑ̃ se ʒuʁ si ‖]

750

EN Nadya used to have a piano, but she sold it a few years ago.

FR Nadya avait un piano, mais elle l'a vendu il y a quelques années.
IPA [(...) avε t‿œ̃ pjano | mε εl l‿a vɑ̃dy i l‿i a kεl k‿ane ‖]

751

EN When I was a child, I didn't use to like mushrooms.

FR Quand j'étais un enfant, je n'aimais pas les champignons.
IPA [kɑ̃ ʒ‿ete œ̃ n‿ɑ̃fɑ̃ | ʒø n‿εmε pa le ʃɑ̃piɲɔ̃ ‖]

752

EN Where did you use to live before you came here?

FR Où habitais-tu avant de venir ici?
IPA [u abitɛ ty avã dø v°niʁ isi ‖]

753

EN He used to play baseball.

FR Il jouait au baseball.
IPA [il ʒwɛ o bezbol ‖]

754

EN He used to be a taxi driver.

FR Il était chauffeur de taxi.
IPA [i l‿etɛ ʃofœʁ dø taksi ‖]

755

EN They used to live in the country.

FR Ils (♀elles) habitaient à la campagne.
IPA [il (♀ɛl) abitɛ a la kãpaɲ ‖]

756

EN I used to wear glasses.

FR Je portais des lunettes.
IPA [ʒø pɔʁtɛ de lynɛt ‖]

757

EN This building used to be a hotel.

FR Ce bâtiment était un hôtel.
IPA [sø batimã etɛ t‿œ̃ n‿otɛl ‖]

758

EN Do you play sports? — No, I used to swim every day though.

FR Fais-tu du sport? — Non, mais j'avais l'habitude de nager tous les jours.
IPA [fɛ ty dy spɔʁ ‖ — nɔ̃ | mɛ ʒ‿avɛ l‿abityd dø naʒe tu le ʒuʁ ‖]

759

EN Do you go out much? — No, I used to go out three (3) nights a week though.

FR Sors-tu souvent? — Non, mais j'avais l'habitude de sortir trois soirs par semaine.
IPA [sɔʁ ty suvã ‖ — nɔ̃ | mɛ ʒ‿avɛ l‿abityd dø sɔʁtiʁ tʁwa swaʁ paʁ s°mɛn ‖]

760

EN Do you play any instruments? — No, I used to play guitar though.

FR Joues-tu d'un instrument? — Non, mais j'ai déjà joué de la guitare.
IPA [ʒu ty d‿œ̃ ɛ̃stʁymã ‖ — nɔ̃ | mɛ ʒ‿ɛ deʒa ʒwe dø la gitaʁ ‖]

761

EN Do you like to read? — I don't have the time, but I used to read a lot.

FR Aimes-tu lire? — Je n'ai pas le temps, mais j'avais l'habitude de lire beaucoup.

IPA [ɛm ty liʁ || — ʒø n‿ɛ pa lø tɑ̃ | mɛ ʒ‿avɛ l‿abityd dø liʁ boku ||]

762

EN Do you travel much? — I'd like to. I used to travel several times a year though.

FR Voyages-tu beaucoup? — J'aimerais ça. J'avais l'habitude de voyager plusieurs fois par année.

IPA [vwajaʒ ty boku || — ʒ‿ɛmˈʁɛ sa || ʒ‿avɛ l‿abityd dø vwajaʒe plyzjœʁ fwa pa ʁ‿ane ||]

763

EN I used to play tennis, but I stopped playing a few years ago.

FR Je jouais au tennis, mais j'ai arrêté de jouer il y a quelques années.

IPA [ʒø ʒwɛ o tenis | mɛ ʒ‿ɛ aʁete dø ʒwe ʁ‿i l‿i a kɛl k‿ane ||]

764

EN Do you play any sports? — Yes, I play basketball.

FR Pratiques-tu un sport? — Oui, je joue au basketball.

IPA [pʁatik ty œ̃ spoʁ || — wi | ʒø ʒu o (...) ||]

765

EN Do you have a car? — No, I used to have one (1), but I sold it.

FR As-tu une voiture? — Non, j'en avais une, mais je l'ai vendue.

IPA [a ty yn vwatyʁ ‖ — nɔ̃ | ʒ‿ɑ̃ avɛ z‿yn | mɛ ʒø l‿ɛ vɑ̃dy ‖]

766

EN Igor used to be a waiter. Now he's the manager of a hotel.

FR Igor était serveur. Maintenant, il est gérant d'hôtel.

IPA [(...) etɛ sɛʁvœʁ ‖ mɛ̃tⁿnɑ̃ | i l‿e ʒeʁɑ̃ d‿otɛl ‖]

767

EN Do you go to work by car? — Sometimes, but most days I go by subway.

FR Vas-tu au travail en voiture? — Parfois, mais la plupart du temps, j'y vais en train.

IPA [va ty o tʁavaj ɑ̃ vwatyʁ ‖ — paʁfwa | mɛ la plypaʁ dy tɑ̃ | ʒ‿i vɛ z‿ɑ̃ tʁɛ̃ ‖]

768

EN When I was a child, I never used to eat meat, but I eat it now.

FR Quand j'étais un enfant, je ne mangeais pas de viande, mais j'en mange maintenant.

IPA [kɑ̃ ʒ‿etɛ œ̃ n‿ɑ̃fɑ̃ | ʒø nø mɑ̃ʒɛ pa dø vjɑd | mɛ ʒ‿ɑ̃ mɑ̃ʒ mɛ̃t°nɑ̃ ||]

769

EN Angela loves to watch TV. She watches it every night.

FR Angela adore regarder la télé. Elle la regarde tous les soirs.

IPA [(...) adɔʁ ʁ°gaʁde la tele || ɛl la ʁ°gaʁd tu le swaʁ ||]

770

EN We used to live near the airport, but we moved downtown a few years ago.

FR Nous vivions près de l'aéroport, mais nous avons déménagé au centre-ville il y a quelques années.

IPA [nu vivjɔ̃ pʁɛ dø l‿aeʁopɔʁ | mɛ nu z‿avɔ̃ demenaʒe o sɑ̃tʁ°vil i l‿i a kɛl k‿ane ||]

771

EN Normally I start work at seven am (7:00), so I get up very early.

FR Je commence normalement le travail à sept heures (7 h), alors je me lève très tôt.

IPA [ʒø komãs nɔʁmal°mã lø tʁavaj a sɛ t‿œʁ (7 h) | alɔʁ ʒø mø lɛv tʁɛ to ||]

772

EN What games did you use to play when you were a child?

FR À quels jeux jouais-tu lorsque tu étais un enfant?

IPA [a kɛl ʒø ʒwɛ ty lɔʁsk° ty ete z‿œ̃ n‿ɑ̃fɑ̃ ||]

773

EN Have you been to France? — No, I haven't.

FR Es-tu déjà allé en France? — Non, je n'y suis jamais allé.

IPA [ɛ ty deʒa ale ɑ̃ fʁɑs || — nɔ̃ | ʒø n‿i sɥi ʒamɛ z‿ale ||]

774

EN We've been to Canada, but we haven't been to Alaska.

FR Nous sommes allés (♀ allées) au Canada, mais nous ne sommes jamais allés (♀ allées) en Alaska.

IPA [nu sɔm ale (♀ ale) o kanada | mɛ nu nø sɔm ʒamɛ z‿ale (♀ ale) ɑ̃ alaska ||]

775

EN Shakira's an interesting person. She's had many different jobs and has lived in many places.

FR Shakira est une personne intéressante. Elle a eu plusieurs emplois différents et vécu à plusieurs endroits.

IPA [(...) e t‿yn pɛʁsɔn ɛ̃teʁɛsɑ̃t ‖ ɛ l‿a y plyzjœ ʁ‿ɑ̃plwa difeʁɑ̃ e veky a plyzjœ ʁ‿ɑ̃dʁwa ‖‖]

776

EN I've seen that man before, but I can't remember where.

FR J'ai déjà vu cet homme, mais je ne me souviens pas où.

IPA [ʒ‿ɛ deʒa vy sɛ t‿ɔm | mɛ ʒø nø mø suvjɛ̃ pa z‿u ‖‖]

777

EN How many times has Brazil won the World Cup?

FR Combien de fois le Brésil a-t-il gagné la Coupe du monde?

IPA [kɔ̃bjɛ̃ dø fwa lø bʁezil a t‿il gaɲe la kup dy mɔ̃d ‖‖]

778

EN Have you read this book? — Yes, I've read it twice.

FR As-tu déjà lu ce livre? — Oui, je l'ai lu deux fois.

IPA [a ty deʒa ly sø livʁ ‖ — wi | ʒø l‿ɛ ly dø fwa ‖‖]

779

EN Has she ever been to Australia? — Yes, once.

FR Est-elle déjà allée en Australie? — Oui, une fois.
IPA [e t̪ɛl deʒa ale ɑ̃ ostʁali || — wi | yn fwa ||]

780

EN Have you ever played golf? — Yes, I play a lot.

FR As-tu déjà joué au golf? — Oui, je joue souvent.
IPA [a ty deʒa ʒwe o gɔlf || — wi | ʒø ʒu suvɑ̃ ||]

781

EN My sister's never traveled by plane.

FR Ma sœur n'a jamais voyagé en avion.
IPA [ma sœʁ n̪a ʒamɛ vwajaʒe ɑ̃ n̪avjɔ̃ ||]

782

EN I've never ridden a horse.

FR Je ne suis jamais monté à cheval.
IPA [ʒø nø sɥi ʒamɛ mɔ̃te a ʃ°val ||]

783

EN Who is that man? — I don't know, I've never seen
him before.

FR Qui est cet homme? — Je ne sais pas, je ne l'ai
jamais vu.
IPA [ki e sɛ t̪ɔm || — ʒø nø sɛ pa | ʒø nø l̪ɛ ʒamɛ vy ||]

784

EN Have you ever been to Montreal? — No, never.

FR Es-tu déjà allé (♀ allée) à Montréal? — Non, jamais.
IPA [ɛ ty deʒa ale (♀ ale) a mɔ̃ʁeal ‖ — nɔ̃ | ʒamɛ ‖]

785

EN Have you ever played golf? — No, never.

FR As-tu déjà joué au golf? — Non, jamais.
IPA [a ty deʒa ʒwe o ɡɔlf ‖ — nɔ̃ | ʒamɛ ‖]

786

EN Have you ever been to South Korea? — Yes, once.

FR Es-tu déjà allé (♀ allée) en Corée du Sud? — Oui, une fois.
IPA [ɛ ty deʒa ale (♀ ale) ɑ̃ kɔʁe dy syd ‖ — wi | yn fwa ‖]

787

EN Have you ever lost your passport? — No, never.

FR As-tu déjà perdu ton passeport? — Non, jamais.
IPA [a ty deʒa pɛʁdy tɔ̃ paspɔʁ ‖ — nɔ̃ | ʒamɛ ‖]

788
EN Have you ever flown in a helicopter? — No, never.

FR As-tu déjà volé à bord d'un hélicoptère? — Non, jamais.
IPA [a ty deʒa vole a bɔʁ d‿œ̃ elikɔptɛʁ || — nɔ̃ | ʒamɛ ||]

789
EN Have you ever won a race? — Yes, a few times.

FR As-tu déjà gagné une course? — Oui, quelques fois.
IPA [a ty deʒa gaɲe yn kuʁs || — wi | kɛlk fwa ||]

790
EN Have you ever been to Peru? — Yes, twice.

FR Es-tu déjà allé (♀ allée) au Pérou? — Oui, deux fois.
IPA [ɛ ty deʒa ale (♀ ale) o peʁu || — wi | dø fwa ||]

791
EN Have you ever driven a bus? — No, never.

FR As-tu déjà conduit un autobus? — Non, jamais.
IPA [a ty deʒa kɔ̃dɥi t‿œ̃ n‿otobys || — nɔ̃ | ʒamɛ ||]

792
EN Have you ever broken your leg? — Yes, once.

FR T'es-tu déjà cassé une jambe? — Oui, une fois.
IPA [t‿ɛ ty deʒa kase yn ʒɑ̃b || — wi | yn fwa ||]

793

EN She's been to Spain twice.

FR Elle est allée en Espagne deux fois.

IPA [ɛ l̩e t̩ale ɑ̃ espagne dø fwa ||]

794

EN She's been to Japan once.

FR Elle est allée au Japon une fois.

IPA [ɛ l̩e t̩ale o ʒapɔ̃ yn fwa ||]

795

EN She's won a race several times.

FR Elle a déjà gagné plusieurs courses.

IPA [ɛ l̩a deʒa gaɲe plyzjœʁ kuʁs ||]

796

EN She's never flown in a helicopter.

FR Elle n'a jamais volé à bord d'un hélicoptère.

IPA [ɛl n̩a ʒamɛ vole a bɔʁ d̩œ̃ elikɔptɛʁ ||]

797

EN I've been to New York once.

FR Je suis déjà allé (♀allée) à New York une fois.

IPA [ʒø sɥi deʒa ale (♀ale) a nuw jɔʁk yn fwa ||]

798

EN I've never played tennis.

FR Je n'ai jamais joué au tennis.
IPA [ʒø n‿ɛ ʒamɛ ʒwe o tenis ‖]

799

EN I've never driven a truck.

FR Je n'ai jamais conduit un camion.
IPA [ʒø n‿ɛ ʒamɛ kɔ̃dɥi t‿œ̃ kamjɔ̃ ‖]

800

EN I've been late for school several times.

FR J'ai déjà été en retard à l'école plusieurs fois.
IPA [ʒ‿ɛ deʒa ete ɑ̃ ʁə̀taʁ a l‿ekɔl plyzjœʁ fwa ‖]

GMS #801 - 900

801

EN She's had many different jobs.

FR Elle a eu plusieurs emplois différents.
IPA [ɛ l̪a y plyzjœ ʁ‿ɑ̃plwa difeʁɑ̃ ‖]

802

EN She's written ten (10) books.

FR Elle a écrit dix livres.
IPA [ɛ l̪a ekʁi dis livʁ ‖]

803

EN She's written a lot of interesting things.

FR Elle a écrit des tas de choses intéressantes.
IPA [ɛ l̪a ekʁi de ta dø ʃoz ɛ̃teʁɛsɑ̃t ‖]

804

EN She's traveled all over the world.

FR Elle a voyagé partout autour du monde.
IPA [ɛ l̪a vwajaʒe paʁtu t‿otuʁ dy mɔ̃d ‖]

805

EN She's been married three (3) times.

FR Elle a été mariée trois fois.
IPA [ε l̩a ete maʁje tʁwa fwa |||]

806

EN She's met a lot of interesting people.

FR Elle a rencontré des tas de gens intéressants.
IPA [ε l̩a ʁãkɔ̃tʁe de ta dø ʒã ɛ̃teʁɛsã |||]

807

EN I've seen that woman before, but I can't remember her name.

FR J'ai déjà vu cette femme, mais je ne me souviens pas de son nom.
IPA [ʒ‿ɛ deʒa vy sɛt fam | me ʒø nø mø suvjɛ̃ pa dø sɔ̃ nɔ̃ |||]

808

EN Have you ever played basketball? — Just once.

FR As-tu déjà joué au basketball? — Juste une fois.
IPA [a ty deʒa ʒwe o (...) || — ʒyst yn fwa |||]

809

EN Have you ever written a poem? — Yes, in high school.

FR As-tu déjà écrit un poème? — Oui, au lycée.

IPA [a ty deʒa ekʁi t‿œ̃ poɛm || — wi | o lise ||]

810

EN Does she know Claude? — No, she's never met him.

FR Connaît-elle Claude? — Non, elle ne l'a jamais rencontré.

IPA [konɛ t‿ɛl (...) || — nɔ̃ | ɛl nø l‿a ʒamɛ ʁɑ̃kɔ̃tʁe ||]

811

EN They have lots of books, and have read all of them.

FR Ils (♀elles) ont des tas de livres, et je les ai tous lus.

IPA [il (♀ɛl) ɔ̃ de ta dø livʁ | e ʒø le z‿ɛ tu ly ||]

812

EN I've never been to New Zealand, but my brother's been there twice.

FR Je ne suis jamais allé (♀allée) en Nouvelle-Zélande, mais mon frère y est allé deux fois.

IPA [ʒø nø sɥi ʒamɛ z‿ale (♀ale) ɑ̃ nuvɛl zeland | mɛ mɔ̃ fʁɛʁ i e ale dø fwa ||]

813

EN Gunter's favorite movie is Star Wars. He's seen it twenty (20) times, but I've never seen it.

FR Le film préféré de Gunter est Star Wars. Il l'a vu vingt fois, mais je ne l'ai jamais vu.

IPA [lø film pʁefeʁe dø (...) e (...) || il l‿a vy vɛ̃ fwa | mɛ ʒø nø l‿ɛ ʒamɛ vy ||]

814

EN I've traveled by plane, bus, and train. Someday, I want to take a trip by boat.

FR J'ai voyagé en avion, en autobus et en train. Un jour, je veux voyager en bateau.

IPA [ʒ‿ɛ vwajaʒe ɑ̃ n‿avjɔ̃ | ɑ̃ n‿otobys e ɑ̃ tʁɛ̃ || œ̃ ʒuʁ | ʒø vø vwajaʒe ʁ‿ɑ̃ bato ||]

815

EN Caroline's on vacation in Brazil. She's there now.

FR Caroline est en vacances au Brésil. Elle est là-bas en ce moment.

IPA [(...) e t‿ɑ̃ vakɑ̃s o bʁezil || ɛ l‿e laba z‿ɑ̃ sø momɑ̃ ||]

816

EN She arrived in Brazil on Monday. Today's Thursday.

FR Elle est arrivée au Brésil lundi. Aujourd'hui est jeudi.

IPA [ɛ l‿e t‿aʁive o bʁezil lœ̃di || oʒuʁdɥi e ʒødi ||]

817

EN How long has she been in Brazil?

FR Depuis quand est-elle au Brésil?
IPA [dᵒpɥi kɑ̃ e t‿ɛl o bʁezil ‖]

818

EN She's been in Brazil since Monday.

FR Elle est au Brésil depuis lundi.
IPA [ɛ l‿e o bʁezil dᵒpɥi lœ̃di ‖]

819

EN She's been in Brazil for three (3) days.

FR Elle est au Brésil depuis trois jours.
IPA [ɛ l‿e o bʁezil dᵒpɥi tʁwa ʒuʁ ‖]

820

EN Emil and Larisa are married. They've been married for five (5) years.

FR Emil et Larisa sont mariés. Ils sont mariés depuis cinq ans.
IPA [(...) e (...) sɔ̃ maʁje ‖ il sɔ̃ maʁje dᵒpɥi sɛ̃ k‿ɑ̃ ‖]

821

EN Are you married? How long have you been married?

FR Es-tu marié (♀mariée)? Depuis quand es-tu marié (♀mariée)?

IPA [ɛ ty maʁje (♀maʁje) || dᵒpɥi kɑ̃ ɛ ty maʁje (♀maʁje) ||]

822

EN Do you know her? How long have you known her?

FR La connais-tu? Depuis quand la connais-tu?

IPA [la konɛ ty || dᵒpɥi kɑ̃ la konɛ ty ||]

823

EN I know Charlotte. I've known her for a long time.

FR Je connais Charlotte. Je la connais depuis longtemps.

IPA [ʒø konɛ (...) || ʒø la konɛ dᵒpɥi lɔ̃tɑ̃ ||]

824

EN Karla lives in Tokyo. How long has she lived in Tokyo?

FR Karla vit à Tokyo. Depuis combien de temps vit-elle à Tokyo?

IPA [(...) vi a (...) || dᵒpɥi kɔ̃bjɛ̃ dø tɑ̃ vi t‿ɛl a (...) ||]

825

EN She's lived there all her life.

FR Elle a vécu là-bas toute sa vie.
IPA [ɛ l̪a veky laba tut sa vi ‖]

826

EN I have a car. How long have you had your car?

FR J'ai une voiture. Depuis combien de temps as-tu ta voiture?
IPA [ʒ̪ɛ yn vwatyʁ ‖ dᵒpɥi kɔ̃bjɛ̃ dø tɑ̃ a ty ta vwatyʁ ‖]

827

EN I've had it since April.

FR Je l'ai depuis avril.
IPA [ʒø l̪ɛ dᵒpɥi z̪avʁil ‖]

828

EN I'm studying German. — How long have you been studying German?

FR J'étudie l'allemand. Depuis combien de temps étudies-tu l'allemand?
IPA [ʒ̪etydi l̪alᵒmɑ̃ ‖ dᵒpɥi kɔ̃bjɛ̃ dø tɑ̃ etydi ty l̪alᵒmɑ̃ ‖]

829

EN I've been studying German for two (2) years.

FR J'étudie l'allemand depuis deux ans.
IPA [ʒ‿etydi l̩alᵊmɑ̃ dᵊpɥi dø z‿ɑ̃ ‖]

830

EN Gerard's watching TV. How long has he been watching TV?

FR Gerard regarde la télé. Depuis combien de temps regarde-t-il la télé?
IPA [(...) ʁᵊgaʁd la tele ‖ dᵊpɥi kɔ̃bjɛ̃ dø tɑ̃ ʁᵊgaʁd t‿il la tele ‖]

831

EN He's been watching TV since five [o'clock] (5:00).

FR Il regarde la télé depuis dix-sept heures (17 h).
IPA [il ʁᵊgaʁd la tele dᵊpɥi disɛ t‿œʁ (17 h) ‖]

832

EN It's raining. It's been raining all day.

FR Il pleut. Il a plu toute la journée.
IPA [il plø ‖ i l̩a ply tut la ʒuʁne ‖]

833

EN Svetlana and Maksim are married. They've been married since nineteen ninety-nine (1999).

FR Svetlana et Maksim sont mariés. Ils sont mariés depuis mille neuf cent quatre-vingt-dix-neuf (1999).

IPA [(...) e (...) sɔ̃ maʁje ‖ il sɔ̃ maʁje dᵊpɥi mil nœf sã katʁᵊvẽdiznœf (1999) ‖]

834

EN Severo's sick. He's been sick for the last few days.

FR Severo est malade. Il est malade depuis quelques jours.

IPA [(...) e malad ‖ i l̺e malad dᵊpɥi kɛlk ʒuʁ ‖]

835

EN We live on Main Street. We've lived there for a long time.

FR Nous vivons sur la rue principale. Nous vivons là depuis longtemps.

IPA [nu vivɔ̃ syʁ la ʁy pʁẽsipal ‖ nu vivɔ̃ la dᵊpɥi lɔ̃tã ‖]

836

EN Florentine works in a bank. She's worked in a bank for five (5) years.

FR Florentine travaille dans une banque. Elle travaille dans une banque depuis cinq ans.

IPA [(...) tʁavaj dã z̺yn bãk ‖ ɛl tʁavaj dã z̺yn bãk dᵊpɥi sẽ k̺ã ‖]

837

EN Hubert has a headache. He's had a headache since he got up this morning.

FR Hubert a mal à la tête. Il a mal à la tête depuis qu'il s'est levé ce matin.

IPA [(...) a mal a la tɛt || i l̪a mal a la tɛt dᵊpɥi k̪il s̪e lᵊve sø matɛ̃ ||]

838

EN I'm studying English. I've studied English for six (6) months.

FR J'étudie l'anglais. J'étudie l'anglais depuis six mois.

IPA [ʒ̪etydi l̪ãglɛ || ʒ̪etydi l̪ãglɛ dᵊpɥi sis mwa ||]

839

EN How long have they been in Brazil?

FR Depuis quand sont-ils (♀ elles) au Brésil?

IPA [dᵊpɥi kã sɔ̃ t̪il (♀ ɛl) o bʁezil ||]

840

EN How long have you known Olivia?

FR Depuis quand connais-tu Olivia?

IPA [dᵊpɥi kã konɛ ty (...) ||]

841

EN How long has she studied Italian?

FR Combien de temps a-t-elle étudié l'italien?
IPA [kɔ̃bjɛ̃ dø tɑ̃ a t‿ɛl etydje l‿italjɛ̃ ||]

842

EN How long has he lived in Seattle?

FR Combien de temps a-t-il vécu à Seattle?
IPA [kɔ̃bjɛ̃ dø tɑ̃ a t‿il veky a (...) ||]

843

EN How long have you been a teacher?

FR Depuis quand es-tu enseignant?
IPA [dᵒpɥi kɑ̃ ɛ ty ɑ̃sɛɲɑ̃ ||]

844

EN How long has it been raining?

FR Depuis quand pleut-il?
IPA [dᵒpɥi kɑ̃ plø t‿il ||]

845

EN They've been married for ten (10) years.

FR Ils sont mariés depuis dix ans.
IPA [il sɔ̃ maʁje dᵒpɥi di z‿ɑ̃ ||]

846

EN Leonardo's lived in Canada since April.

FR Leonardo vit au Canada depuis avril.
IPA [(...) vi o kanada dᵊpɥi z‿avʁil ||]

847

EN Giselle and I are friends. I know her very well.

FR Giselle et moi sommes amis (♀amies). Je la connais très bien.
IPA [(...) e mwa sɔm ami (♀ami) || ʒø la konɛ tʁɛ bjɛ̃ ||]

848

EN Luisa and I are friends. I've known her for a long time.

FR Luisa et moi sommes amis (♀amies). Je la connais depuis longtemps.
IPA [(...) e mwa sɔm ami (♀ami) || ʒø la konɛ dᵊpɥi lɔ̃tɑ̃ ||]

849

EN Sorry I'm late. How long have you been waiting?

FR Désolé, je suis en retard. Depuis quand m'attends-tu?
IPA [dezole | ʒø sɥi z‿ɑ̃ ʁᵊtaʁ || dᵊpɥi kɑ̃ m‿atɑ̃ ty ||]

850

EN Jean works in a hotel now. He likes his job a lot.

FR Jean travaille dans un hôtel maintenant. Il aime beaucoup son travail.

IPA [(...) tʁavaj dɑ̃ z‿œ̃ n‿otɛl mɛ̃t°nɑ̃ || i l‿ɛm boku sɔ̃ tʁavaj ||]

851

EN Isabelle's reading the newspaper. She's been reading it for two (2) hours.

FR Isabelle lit le journal. Elle le lit depuis deux heures.

IPA [(...) li lø ʒuʁnal || ɛl lø li d°pɥi dø z‿œʁ ||]

852

EN How long have you lived in this house?

FR Depuis quand vis-tu dans cette maison?

IPA [d°pɥi kɑ̃ vis ty dɑ̃ sɛt mɛzɔ̃ ||]

853

EN Is that a new coat? — No, I've had this coat for a long time.

FR Est-ce un nouveau manteau? — Non, j'ai ce manteau depuis longtemps.

IPA [ɛs° œ̃ nuvo mɑ̃to || — nɔ̃ | ʒ‿ɛ sø mɑ̃to d°pɥi lɔ̃tɑ̃ ||]

854

EN Maalik's in Seattle right now. He's been there for the last three (3) days.

FR Maalik est à Seattle en ce moment. Il est là-bas depuis trois jours.

IPA [malik e a (...) ɑ̃ sø momɑ̃ || i l̩e laba dᵊpɥi tʁwa ʒuʁ ||]

855

EN Yasmin's in Brazil. She's been there for three (3) days.

FR Yasmin est au Brésil. Elle est là-bas depuis trois jours.

IPA [(...) e o bʁezil || ɛ l̩e laba dᵊpɥi tʁwa ʒuʁ ||]

856

EN Today's Wednesday. She's been there since Monday.

FR Aujourd'hui est mercredi. Elle est là-bas depuis lundi.

IPA [oʒuʁdɥi e mɛʁkʁᵊdi || ɛ l̩e laba dᵊpɥi lœ̃di ||]

857

EN Lucien has been in Canada for six (6) months.

FR Lucien est au Canada depuis six mois.

IPA [(...) e o kanada dᵊpɥi sis mwa ||]

858

EN Lucien has been in Canada since January.

FR Lucien est au Canada depuis janvier.
IPA [(...) e o kanada dᵊpɥi ʒɑ̃vje ‖]

859

EN We've been waiting for two (2) hours.

FR Nous attendons depuis maintenant deux heures.
IPA [nu z‿atɑ̃dɔ̃ dᵊpɥi mɛ̃tᵊnɑ̃ dø z‿œʁ ‖]

860

EN We've been waiting since nine [o'clock] (9:00).

FR Nous attentons depuis neuf heures.
IPA [nu attentons dᵊpɥi nœ v‿œʁ ‖]

861

EN I've lived in Chicago for a long time.

FR Je vis à Chicago depuis longtemps.
IPA [ʒø vis a (...) dᵊpɥi lɔ̃tɑ̃ ‖]

862

EN I've lived in Chicago since I was ten (10) years old.

FR Je vis à Chicago depuis que j'ai dix ans.
IPA [ʒø vis a (...) dᵊpɥi kø ʒ‿ɛ di z‿ɑ̃ ‖]

863

EN Jasmine started her new job three (3) weeks ago.

FR Jasmine a commencé son nouveau travail il y a trois semaines.

IPA [(...) a komãse sɔ̃ nuvo tʁavaj i l̨i a tʁwa sᵊmɛn ‖]

864

EN When did Noboru leave? — He left ten (10) minutes ago.

FR Quand Noboru est-il parti? — Il est parti il y a dix minutes.

IPA [kã (...) e t̨il paʁti ‖ — i l̨e paʁti i l̨i a dis minyt ‖]

865

EN I had dinner an hour ago.

FR J'ai dîné il y a une heure.

IPA [ʒ̨ɛ dine i l̨i a yn œʁ ‖]

866

EN Life was very different a hundred (100) years ago.

FR La vie était très différente il y a cent ans.

IPA [la vi etɛ tʁɛ difeʁãt i l̨i a sã t̨ã ‖]

867

EN When did Michiko arrive in Brazil?

FR Quand Michiko est-elle arrivée au Brésil?
IPA [kɑ̃ (...) e t̪ɛl aʁive o bʁezil ‖]

868

EN She arrived in Brazil three (3) days ago.

FR Elle est arrivée il y a trois jours.
IPA [ɛ l̪e t̪aʁive i l̪i a tʁwa ʒuʁ ‖]

869

EN How long has she been in Brazil?

FR Depuis quand est-elle au Brésil?
IPA [d°pɥi kɑ̃ e t̪ɛl o bʁezil ‖]

870

EN She's been in Brazil for three (3) days.

FR Elle est au Brésil depuis trois jours.
IPA [ɛ l̪e o bʁezil d°pɥi tʁwa ʒuʁ ‖]

871

EN My aunt has lived in Australia for fifteen (15) years.

FR Ma tante vit en Australie depuis quinze ans.
IPA [ma tɑ̃t vi t̪ɑ̃ ostʁali d°pɥi kɛ̃z ɑ̃ ‖]

872

EN Lilianne's in her office. She's been there since seven [o'clock] (7:00).

FR Lilianne est dans son bureau. Elle y est depuis sept heures (7 h).

IPA [(...) e dã sõ byʁo ‖ ɛ l̩i e dᵊpɥi sɛ t̯œʁ (7 h) ‖]

873

EN Mexico has been an independent country since eighteen twenty-one (1821).

FR Le Mexique est un pays indépendant depuis mille huit cent vingt et un (1821).

IPA [lø meksik e t̯œ̃ pei ɛ̃depãdã dᵊpɥi mil ɥit sã vɛ̃ e œ̃ (1821) ‖]

874

EN The bus is late. We've been waiting for twenty (20) minutes.

FR L'autobus est en retard. Nous l'attendons depuis vingt minutes.

IPA [l̩otobys e t̯ã ʁᵊtaʁ ‖ nu l̩atãdõ dᵊpɥi vɛ̃ minyt ‖]

875

EN Nobody lives in those houses. They've been empty for many years.

FR Personne ne vit dans ces maisons. Elles sont vacantes depuis plusieurs années.

IPA [pɛʁsɔn nø vi dɑ̃ se mɛzɔ̃ ‖ ɛl sɔ̃ vakɑ̃t dᵊpɥi plyzjœ ʁ‿ane ‖]

876

EN Michel's been sick for a long time. He's been in the hospital since October of last year.

FR Michel est malade depuis longtemps. Il est à l'hôpital depuis le mois d'octobre de l'an dernier.

IPA [(...) e malad dᵊpɥi lɔ̃tɑ̃ ‖ i l‿e a l‿opital dᵊpɥi lø mwa d‿ɔktɔbʁ dø l‿ɑ̃ dɛʁnje ‖]

877

EN When was the last time you ate? — Three hours ago.

FR Quand as-tu mangé pour la dernière fois? — Il y a trois heures.

IPA [kɑ̃ a ty mɑ̃ʒe puʁ la dɛʁnjɛʁ fwa ‖ — i l‿i a tʁwa z‿œʁ ‖]

878

EN When was the last time you were sick? — Five months ago.

FR Quand as-tu été malade pour la dernière fois? — Il y a cinq mois.

IPA [kɑ̃ a ty ete malad puʁ la dɛʁnjɛʁ fwa || — i l̪i a sɛ̃k mwa ||]

879

EN When was the last time you went to the movies? — Just last week.

FR Quand es-tu allé (♀ allée) au cinéma pour la dernière fois? — La semaine dernière.

IPA [kɑ̃ ɛ ty ale (♀ ale) o sinema puʁ la dɛʁnjɛʁ fwa || — la sᵊmɛn dɛʁnjɛʁ ||]

880

EN When was the last time you were in a car? — Just this morning.

FR Quand as-tu été dans une voiture pour la dernière fois? — Ce matin.

IPA [kɑ̃ a ty ete dɑ̃ z‿yn vwatyʁ puʁ la dɛʁnjɛʁ fwa || — sø matɛ̃ ||]

881

EN When was the last time you went on vacation? — A year ago.

FR Quand es-tu allé (♀allée) en vacances pour la dernière fois? — Il y a un an.

IPA [kɑ̃ ɛ ty ale (♀ale) ɑ̃ vakɑ̃s puʁ la dɛʁnjɛʁ fwa || — i l̪ i a œ̃ n̪ɑ̃ ||]

882

EN Mungeol and Weonhye have been married for twenty (20) years.

FR Mungeol et Weonhye sont mariés depuis vingt ans.

IPA [(...) e (...) sɔ̃ maʁje dᵊpɥi vɛ̃ t̪ɑ̃ ||]

883

EN Mungeol and Weonhye got married twenty (20) years ago.

FR Mungeol et Weonhye se sont mariés il y a vingt ans.

IPA [(...) e (...) sø sɔ̃ maʁje z̪ i l̪ i a vɛ̃ t̪ɑ̃ ||]

884

EN Nicholas arrived an hour ago.

FR Nicholas est arrivé il y a une heure.

IPA [(...) e t̪ aʁive i l̪ i a yn œʁ ||]

885

EN I bought these shoes a few days ago.

FR J'ai acheté ces chaussures il y a quelques jours.
IPA [ʒ‿ɛ aʃˤte se ʃosyʁ i l‿i a kɛlk ʒuʁ ‖]

886

EN Miriam's been studying English for six (6) months.

FR Miriam étudie l'anglais depuis six mois.
IPA [(...) etydi l‿ɑ̃glɛ dˤpɥi sis mwa ‖]

887

EN Have you known Heuijeong for a long time?

FR Connais-tu Heuijeong depuis longtemps?
IPA [konɛ ty (...) dˤpɥi lɔ̃tɑ̃ ‖]

888

EN Natalie's been in Brazil for three (3) days.

FR Natalie est au Brésil depuis trois jours.
IPA [(...) e o bʁezil dˤpɥi tʁwa ʒuʁ ‖]

889

EN Geonhong's been here since Tuesday.

FR Geonhong est ici depuis mardi.
IPA [(...) e isi dˤpɥi maʁdi ‖]

890

EN It's been raining for an hour.

FR Il pleut depuis une heure.
IPA [il plø dᵊpɥi z‿yn œʁ ||]

891

EN I've known Mengjuan since two thousand two (2002).

FR Je connais Mengjuan depuis deux mille deux (2002).
IPA [ʒø konɛ (...) dᵊpɥi dø mil dø (2002) ||]

892

EN Remy and Pauline have been married for six (6) months.

FR Remy et Pauline sont mariés depuis six mois.
IPA [ʁᵊmi e (...) sɔ̃ maʁje dᵊpɥi sis mwa ||]

893

EN Hitomi has studied medicine at the university for three (3) years.

FR Hitomi a étudié la médecine à l'université durant trois ans.
IPA [(...) a etydje la mɛdsin a l‿ynivɛʁsite dyʁɑ̃ tʁwa z‿ɑ̃ ||]

894

EN Ichirou's played the piano since he was seven (7) years old.

FR Ichirou joue du piano depuis qu'il a sept ans.
IPA [(...) ʒu dy pjano dᵊpɥi k‿il a sɛ t‿ɑ̃ ||]

895

EN His car's dirty. He's washing his car. He's washed his car. It's clean now.

FR Sa voiture est sale. Il lave sa voiture. Il a lavé sa voiture. Elle est propre maintenant.
IPA [sa vwatyʁ e sal || il lav sa vwatyʁ || i l‿a lave sa vwatyʁ || ɛ l‿e pʁɔpʁ mɛ̃tᵊnɑ̃ ||]

896

EN They're at home. They're going out. They've gone out. They're not at home now.

FR Ils (♀elles) sont à la maison. Ils (♀elles) s'apprêtent à sortir. Ils (♀elles) sont sortis (♀sorties). Ils (♀elles) ne sont pas à la maison en ce moment.
IPA [il (♀ɛl) sɔ̃ a la mɛzɔ̃ || il (♀ɛl) s‿apʁɛt a sɔʁtiʁ || il (♀ɛl) sɔ̃ sɔʁti (♀sɔʁti) || il (♀ɛl) nø sɔ̃ pa a la mɛzɔ̃ ɑ̃ sø momɑ̃ ||]

897

EN I've lost my passport. I can't find my passport now.

FR J'ai perdu mon passeport. Je n'arrive pas à trouver mon passeport en ce moment.

IPA [ʒ‿ɛ pɛʁdy mɔ̃ paspɔʁ ‖ ʒø n‿aʁiv pa a tʁuve mɔ̃ paspɔʁ ɑ̃ sø momɑ̃ ‖]

898

EN Where's Renee? — She's gone to bed. She's in bed now.

FR Où est Renée? — Elle est allée se coucher. Elle est au lit maintenant.

IPA [u e ʁ°ne ‖ — ɛ l‿e t‿ale sø kuʃe ‖ ɛ l‿e o li mɛ̃t°nɑ̃ ‖]

899

EN We've bought a new car. We have a new car now.

FR Nous avons acheté une nouvelle voiture. Nous avons une nouvelle voiture maintenant.

IPA [nu z‿avɔ̃ aʃ°te yn nuvɛl vwatyʁ ‖ nu z‿avɔ̃ z‿yn nuvɛl vwatyʁ mɛ̃t°nɑ̃ ‖]

900

EN It's Rashmi's birthday tomorrow, and I haven't bought her a present. > I don't have a present for her yet.

FR C'est l'anniversaire de Rashmi demain et je ne lui ai pas acheté de cadeau. Je n'ai pas encore de cadeau pour elle.

IPA [sɛ l̪anivɛʁsɛʁ də (...) d°mɛ̃ n̪e ʒø nø lɥi ɛ pa z̪aʃ°te də kado || ʒø n̪ɛ pa z̪ɑ̃kɔʁ də kado pu ʁ̪ɛl ||]

GMS #901 - 1000

901

EN Junhong is away on vacation. Where has he gone? Where is he now?

FR Junhong est en vacances. Où est-il allé? Où est-il maintenant?

IPA [(...) e t̪ã vakãs || u e t̪il ale || u e t̪il mɛ̃t°nã ||]

902

EN Have you met my brother, or should I introduce you?

FR As-tu rencontré mon frère ou devrais-je vous présenter?

IPA [a ty ʁãkõtʁe mõ fʁɛʁ u d°vʁɛ ʒø vu pʁezãte ||]

903

EN I was a very slow typist in college, but I've gotten faster.

FR J'écrivais lentement à l'université, mais j'écris plus vite maintenant.

IPA [ʒ̪ekʁivɛ lãt°mã a l̪ynivɛʁsite | mɛ ʒ̪ekʁi plys vit mɛ̃t°nã ||]

904

EN Where's your key? — I've lost it. I lost it.

FR Où est ta clé? — Je l'ai perdue.
IPA [u e ta kle || — ʒø l̩ɛ pɛʁdy ||]

905

EN Is Oliver here? — No, he's gone home. He went home.

FR Est-ce qu'Oliver est ici? — Non, il est rentré à la maison.
IPA [ɛsᵊ k (...) e isi || — nɔ̃ | i l̩e ʁɑ̃tʁe a la mɛzɔ̃ ||]

906

EN We've bought a new car. We bought a new car.

FR Nous avons acheté une nouvelle voiture.
IPA [nu z̩avɔ̃ aʃᵊte yn nuvɛl vwatyʁ ||]

907

EN I lost my keys yesterday.

FR J'ai perdu mes clés hier.
IPA [ʒ̩ɛ pɛʁdy me kle jɛʁ ||]

908

EN I lost my keys last week.

FR J'ai perdu mes clés la semaine dernière.
IPA [ʒ̩ɛ pɛʁdy me kle la sᵊmɛn dɛʁnjɛʁ ||]

909

EN I've lost my keys five (5) times this month.

FR J'ai perdu mes clés cinq fois ce mois-ci.
IPA [ʒ‿ɛ pɛʁdy me kle sɛ̃k fwa sə mwa si ‖]

910

EN We bought a new car yesterday.

FR Nous avons acheté une nouvelle voiture hier.
IPA [nu z‿avɔ̃ aʃᵊte yn nuvɛl vwatyʁ jɛʁ ‖]

911

EN We bought a new car last week.

FR Nous avons acheté une nouvelle voiture la semaine dernière.
IPA [nu z‿avɔ̃ aʃᵊte yn nuvɛl vwatyʁ la sᵊmɛn dɛʁnjɛʁ ‖]

912

EN We've bought two (2) new cars in the last three (3) years.

FR Nous avons acheté deux nouvelles voitures dans les trois dernières années.
IPA [nu z‿avɔ̃ aʃᵊte dø nuvɛl vwatyʁ dɑ̃ le tʁwa dɛʁnjɛ ʁ‿ane ‖]

913

EN Serge isn't here. He went home. > He's already gone home.

FR Serge n'est pas ici. Il est rentré à la maison. Il est déjà rentré à la maison.

IPA [(...) n̩e pa z̩isi || i l̩e ʁɑ̃tʁe a la mɛzɔ̃ || i l̩e deʒa ʁɑ̃tʁe a la mɛzɔ̃ ||]

914

EN I don't need to call them. I wrote them an email. > I've already written them an email.

FR Je n'ai pas besoin de les appeler. Je leur ai écrit un courriel. Je leur ai déjà écrit un courriel.

IPA [ʒø n̩ɛ pa bøzwɛ̃ dø le z̩apᵊle || ʒø lœ ʁ̩ɛ ekʁi t̩ɶ̃ kuʁjɛl || ʒø lœ ʁ̩ɛ deʒa ekʁi t̩ɶ̃ kuʁjɛl ||]

915

EN Sabine's not coming to the party. She broke her arm. > She's broken her arm.

FR Sabine ne vient pas à la fête. Elle s'est cassé un bras.

IPA [(...) nø vjɛ̃ pa a la fɛt || ɛl s̩e kase ɶ̃ bʁa ||]

916

EN My brother and his wife don't live here any more.
They moved to Seattle. > They've moved to Seattle.

FR Mon frère et sa femme ne vivent plus ici. Ils ont
déménagé à Seattle.

IPA [mɔ̃ fʁɛʁ e sa fam nø viv ply s‿isi ‖ i l‿ɔ̃ demenaʒe a
(...) ‖]

917

EN I made a mistake. > I've made a mistake.

FR J'ai fait une erreur.

IPA [ʒ‿ɛ fɛ t‿yn ɛʁœʁ ‖]

918

EN I lost my wallet. > I've lost my wallet.

FR J'ai perdu mon portefeuille.

IPA [ʒ‿ɛ pɛʁdy mɔ̃ pɔʁt°fœj ‖]

919

EN Did you see it anywhere? > Have you seen it
anywhere?

FR L'as-tu vu quelque part?

IPA [l‿a ty vy kɛlk paʁ ‖]

920

EN Did you hear? > Have you heard?

FR As-tu entendu?
IPA [a ty ãtãdy ||]

921

EN Theo got married. > Theo's gotten married.

FR Theo s'est marié.
IPA [(...) s̩e maʁje ||]

922

EN I've done the shopping. > I did the shopping.

FR J'ai fait les courses.
IPA [ʒ̩ɛ fɛ le kuʁs ||]

923

EN Gustavo has taken my bike again without asking. > Gustavo took my bike without asking.

FR Gustavo a encore pris mon vélo sans me le demander. Gustavo a pris mon vélo sans me le demander.
IPA [(...) a ãkɔʁ pʁi mõ velo sã mø lø dᵊmãde || (...) a pʁi mõ velo sã mø lø dᵊmãde ||]

924

EN Have you told your friends the good news? > Did you tell your friends the good news?

FR As-tu annoncé la bonne nouvelle à tes amis (♀ amies)?

IPA [a ty anɔ̃se la bɔn nuvɛl a te z‿ami (♀ ami) ‖]

925

EN We haven't paid the electric bill yet. > We didn't pay the electric bill.

FR Nous n'avons pas encore payé le compte d'électricité. Nous n'avons pas payé le compte d'électricité.

IPA [nu n‿avɔ̃ pa z‿ɑ̃kɔʁ peje lø kɔ̃t d‿elɛktʁisite ‖ nu n‿avɔ̃ pa peje lø kɔ̃t d‿elɛktʁisite ‖]

926

EN Are Vincent and Valerie here? — Yes, they just arrived.

FR Est-ce que Vincent et Valerie sont ici? — Oui, ils viennent d'arriver.

IPA [ɛsᵒ kø (...) e (...) sɔ̃ isi ‖ — wi | il vjɛn d‿aʁive ‖]

927

EN Are you hungry? — No, I just had dinner.

FR As-tu faim? — Non, je viens tout juste de dîner.

IPA [a ty fɛ̃ ‖ — nɔ̃ | ʒø vjɛ̃ tu ʒyst dø dine ‖]

928

EN Is Niraj here? — No, he just left.

FR Est-ce que Niraj est ici? — Non, il vient de partir.
IPA [ɛsᵊ kø (...) e isi || — nɔ̃ | il vjɛ̃ dø paʁtiʁ ||]

929

EN What time are Nikolai and Victoria coming? —
They've already arrived.

FR À quelle heure Nikolai et Victoria viennent-ils? — Ils
sont déjà arrivés.
IPA [a kɛ l‿œʁ (...) e (...) vjɛ n‿il || — il sɔ̃ deʒa aʁive ||]

930

EN It's only nine o'clock (9:00) and Ines has already
gone to bed.

FR Il est seulement vingt et une heures (21 h) et Ines est
déjà au lit.
IPA [i l‿e sœlᵊmɑ̃ vɛ̃ e yn œʁ (21 h) e (...) e deʒa o li ||]

931

EN This is Yvonne. — Yes, we've already met.

FR Voici Yvonne. — Oui, nous nous sommes déjà
rencontrés.
IPA [vwasi yvonne || — wi | nu nu sɔm deʒa ʁɑ̃kɔ̃tʁe ||]

932

EN Are Isidor and Sandra here? — No, they haven't arrived yet.

FR Est-ce qu'Isidor et Sandra sont ici? — Non, ils ne sont pas encore arrivés.

IPA [ɛsᵊ k (...) e (...) sɔ̃ isi || — nɔ̃ | il nø sɔ̃ pa z‿ɑ̃kɔʁ aʁive ||]

933

EN Does Yannick know that you're going away? — No, I haven't told him yet.

FR Yannick sait-il que tu pars? — Non, je ne lui ai pas encore dit.

IPA [(...) sɛ t‿il kø ty paʁ || — nɔ̃ | ʒø nø lɥi ɛ pa z‿ɑ̃kɔʁ di ||]

934

EN Dora has bought a new dress, but she hasn't worn it yet.

FR Dora a acheté une nouvelle robe, mais elle ne l'a pas encore portée.

IPA [(...) a aʃᵊte yn nuvɛl ʁɔb | mɛ ɛl nø l‿a pa z‿ɑ̃kɔʁ pɔʁte ||]

935

EN Have Chandra and Indira arrived yet? — No, not yet. We're still waiting for them.

FR Est-ce que Chandra et Indira sont déjà arrivés? — Non, pas encore. Nous les attendons toujours.

IPA [ɛs° kø (...) e (...) sɔ̃ deʒa aʁive || — nɔ̃ | pa z‿ɑ̃kɔʁ || nu le z‿atɑ̃dɔ̃ tuʒuʁ ||]

936

EN Has Zinaida started her new job yet? — No, she's starting next week.

FR Est-ce que Zinaida a déjà commencé son nouveau travail? — Non, elle commence la semaine prochaine.

IPA [ɛs° kø zinaida a deʒa komɑ̃se sɔ̃ nuvo tʁavaj || — nɔ̃ | ɛl komɑ̃s la s°mɛn pʁoʃɛn ||]

937

EN This is my new dress. — It's nice, have you worn it yet?

FR Voici ma nouvelle robe. — Elle est jolie, l'as-tu déjà portée?

IPA [vwasi ma nuvɛl ʁɔb || — ɛ l̯e ʒoli | l̯a ty deʒa pɔʁte ||]

938

EN What time is Stan arriving? — He's already arrived.

FR À quelle heure Stan arrive-t-il? — Il est déjà arrivé.
IPA [a kɛ l‿œʁ (...) aʁiv t‿il || — i l‿e deʒa aʁive |||]

939

EN Do your friends want to see the movie? — No, they've already seen it.

FR Est-ce que tes amis (♀amies) veulent voir le film? — Non, ils (♀elles) l'ont déjà vu.
IPA [ɛs° kø te z‿ami (♀ami) vœl vwaʁ lø film || — nɔ̃ | il (♀ɛl) l‿ɔ̃ deʒa vy |||]

940

EN Don't forget to call Vadim. — I've already called him.

FR N'oublie pas d'appeler Vadim. — Je l'ai déjà appelé.
IPA [n‿ubli pa d‿ap°le (...) || — ʒø l‿ɛ deʒa ap°le |||]

941

EN When is Hideki going to work? — He's already gone to work.

FR À quelle heure Hideki va-t-il au travail? — Il est déjà parti au travail.
IPA [a kɛ l‿œʁ (...) va t‿il o tʁavaj || — i l‿e deʒa paʁti o tʁavaj |||]

942

EN When does Hanako start her new job? — She's already started it.

FR Quand Hanako commence-t-elle son nouveau travail? — Elle l'a déjà commencé.

IPA [kɑ̃ (...) komɑ̃s t‿ɛl sɔ̃ nuvo tʁavaj || — ɛl l‿a deʒa komɑ̃se ||]

943

EN Has Tamara started her new job yet?

FR Est-ce que Tamara a déjà commencé son nouveau travail?

IPA [ɛsᵊ kø (...) a deʒa komɑ̃se sɔ̃ nuvo tʁavaj ||]

944

EN Have you told your father about the accident yet?

FR As-tu déjà parlé de l'accident à ton père?

IPA [a ty deʒa paʁle dø l‿aksidɑ̃ a tɔ̃ pɛʁ ||]

945

EN I've just eaten a big dinner, so I'm not hungry.

FR Je viens de manger un gros dîner, je n'ai pas faim.

IPA [ʒø vjɛ̃ dø mɑ̃ʒe ʁ‿œ̃ gʁo dine | ʒø n‿ɛ pa fɛ̃ ||]

946

EN Mengxuan can watch TV because she's already done her homework.

FR Mengxuan peut regarder la télé, parce qu'elle a déjà fini ses devoirs.

IPA [(...) pø ʁᵊgaʁde la tele | paʁs k̬ɛl a deʒa fini se dᵊvwaʁ ‖]

947

EN You can't go to bed. You haven't brushed your teeth yet.

FR Tu ne peux pas aller au lit. Tu ne t'es pas encore brossé les dents.

IPA [ty nø pø pa z̬ale o li ‖ ty nø t̬ɛ pa z̬ãkɔʁ bʁose le dã ‖]

948

EN You can't talk to Vladimir because he's just gone home.

FR Tu ne peux pas parler à Vladimir, parce qu'il vient juste de rentrer à la maison.

IPA [ty nø pø pa paʁle a (...) | paʁs k̬il vjɛ̃ ʒyst dø ʁãtʁe a la mɛzɔ̃ ‖]

949

EN Ramona's just gotten out of the hospital, so she can't go to work.

FR Ramona vient de sortir de l'hôpital, alors elle ne peut pas aller au travail.

IPA [(...) vjɛ̃ dø sɔʁtiʁ dø l‿opital | alɔ ʁ‿ɛl nø pø pa z‿ale o tʁavaj ‖]

950

EN Have you given the post office our new address yet?

FR As-tu donné notre nouvelle adresse au bureau de poste?

IPA [a ty done nɔtʁ nuvɛ l‿adʁɛs o byʁo dø pɔst ‖]

951

EN The postman hasn't come yet.

FR Le facteur n'est pas encore passé.

IPA [lø faktœʁ n‿e pa z‿ɑ̃kɔʁ pase ‖]

952

EN I've just spoken to your sister.

FR Je viens de parler à ta sœur.

IPA [ʒø vjɛ̃ dø paʁle a ta sœʁ ‖]

953

EN Has Jianwen bought a new computer yet?

FR Est-ce que Jianwen a acheté un nouvel ordinateur?
IPA [ɛs° kø (...) a aʃ°te œ̃ nuvɛ lˌɔʁdinatœʁ ‖]

954

EN Geonho and Ayeong haven't told anyone they're getting married yet.

FR Geonho et Ayeong n'ont pas dit à personne qu'ils se mariaient.
IPA [(...) e (...) nˌɔ̃ pa di a pɛʁsɔn kˌil sø maʁjɛ ‖]

955

EN We've already done our packing for our trip.

FR Nous avons déjà fait nos valises pour notre voyage.
IPA [nu zˌavɔ̃ deʒa fɛ no valiz puʁ nɔtʁ vwajaʒ ‖]

956

EN I've just swum a mile and I feel great.

FR Je viens de nager un kilomètre et je me sens bien.
IPA [ʒø vjɛ̃ dø naʒe ʁˌœ̃ kilomɛtʁ e ʒø mø sɑ̃s bjɛ̃ ‖]

957

EN Your friend has a new job. Ask her if she has started her new job yet.

FR Ton amie a un nouveau travail. Demande-lui si elle a déjà commencé son nouveau travail.

IPA [tɔ̃ n‿ami a œ̃ nuvo tʁavaj ‖ dᵊmɑ̃d lɥi si ɛ l‿a deʒa komɑ̃se sɔ̃ nuvo tʁavaj ‖]

958

EN Your friend has some new neighbors. Ask him if he has met his new neighbors.

FR Ton ami a de nouveaux voisins. Demande-lui s'il a rencontré ses nouveaux voisins.

IPA [tɔ̃ n‿ami a dø nuvo vwazɛ̃ ‖ dᵊmɑ̃d lɥi s‿il a ʁɑ̃kɔ̃tʁe se nuvo vwazɛ̃ ‖]

959

EN Your friend has to pay her phone bill. Ask her if she has paid her phone bill yet.

FR Ton amie doit payer son compte de téléphone. Demande-lui si elle a déjà payé son compte de téléphone.

IPA [tɔ̃ n‿ami dwa peje sɔ̃ kɔ̃t dø telefɔn ‖ dᵊmɑ̃d lɥi si ɛ l‿a deʒa peje sɔ̃ kɔ̃t dø telefɔn ‖]

960

EN Victor was trying to sell his car. Ask him if he has sold his car yet.

FR Victor essayait de vendre sa voiture. Demande-lui s'il a déjà vendu sa voiture.

IPA [(...) eseje dø vãdʁ sa vwatyʁ || dᵊmãd lɥi s‿il a deʒa vãdy sa vwatyʁ ||]

961

EN I saw Malika yesterday.

FR J'ai vu Malika hier.

IPA [ʒ‿ɛ vy (...) jɛʁ ||]

962

EN Where were you on Sunday afternoon?

FR Où étais-tu dimanche après-midi?

IPA [u etɛ ty dimãʃ apʁɛ midi ||]

963

EN We didn't take a vacation last year.

FR Nous ne sommes pas allés (♀ allées) en vacances l'an dernier.

IPA [nu nø sɔm pa z‿ale (♀ ale) ã vakãs l‿ã dɛʁnje ||]

964

EN What did you do last night? — I stayed at home.

FR Qu'as-tu fait hier soir? — Je suis resté à la maison.
IPA [k‿a ty fɛ jɛʁ swaʁ ‖ — ʒø sɥi ʁeste a la mɛzɔ̃ ‖]

965

EN Shakespeare was a writer and wrote many plays and poems.

FR Shakespeare était un écrivain et il a écrit plusieurs pièces de théâtre et de nombreux poèmes.
IPA [(...) etɛ t‿œ̃ n‿ekʁivɛ̃ e i l‿a ekʁi plyzjœʁ pjɛs dø teatʁ e dø nɔ̃bʁø poɛm ‖]

966

EN When did you buy your computer?

FR Quand as-tu acheté ton ordinateur?
IPA [kɑ̃ a ty aʃ°te tɔ̃ n‿ɔʁdinatœʁ ‖]

967

EN What time did Jamaal go out?

FR À quelle heure Jamaal est-il sorti?
IPA [a kɛ l‿œʁ (...) e t‿il sɔʁti ‖]

968

EN Kenji went home.

FR Kenji est rentré à la maison.
IPA [(...) e ʁɑ̃tʁe a la mɛzɔ̃ ‖]

969

EN Did you have lunch today?

FR As-tu déjeuné aujourd'hui?
IPA [a ty deʒœne oʒuʁdɥi ‖]

970

EN The email didn't arrive at all.

FR Le courriel n'est pas arrivé du tout.
IPA [lø kuʁjɛl n‿e pa z‿aʁive dy tu ‖]

971

EN Have you ever been to Spain? Did you go to Spain last year?

FR Es-tu déjà allé (♀ allée) en Espagne? Es-tu allé (♀ allée) en Espagne l'an dernier?
IPA [ɛ ty deʒa ale (♀ ale) ɑ̃ espagne ‖ ɛ ty ale (♀ ale) ɑ̃ espagne l‿ɑ̃ dɛʁnje ‖]

972

EN My friend has written many books. Shakespeare wrote many plays and poems.

FR Mon ami (♀amie) a écrit plusieurs livres. Shakespeare a écrit plusieurs pièces de théâtre et poèmes.

IPA [mɔ̃ n‿ami (♀ami) a ekʁi plyzjœʁ livʁ ‖ (...) a ekʁi plyzjœʁ pjɛs də teatʁ e poɛm ‖|]

973

EN The email hasn't arrived yet. > The email didn't arrive today.

FR Le courriel n'est pas encore arrivé. Le courriel n'est pas arrivé aujourd'hui.

IPA [lø kuʁjɛl n‿e pa z‿ãkɔʁ aʁive ‖ lø kuʁjɛl n‿e pa z‿aʁive oʒuʁdɥi ‖|]

974

EN We've lived in Paris for six (6) years. > We lived in Paris for six (6) years, but now we live in Rome.

FR Nous avons vécu à Paris pendant six ans. Nous avons vécu à Paris pendant six ans, mais maintenant nous vivons à Rome.

IPA [nu z‿avɔ̃ veky a (...) pãdã si z‿ã ‖ nu z‿avɔ̃ veky a (...) pãdã si z‿ã | mɛ mɛ̃t°nã nu vivɔ̃ a (...) ‖|]

975

EN I had lunch an hour ago.

FR J'ai déjeuné il y a une heure.
IPA [ʒ‿ɛ deʒœne i l‿i a yn œʁ ‖]

976

EN I started my new job last week.

FR J'ai commencé mon nouveau travail la semaine dernière.
IPA [ʒ‿ɛ komɑ̃se mɔ̃ nuvo tʁavaj la sᵊmɛn dɛʁnjɛʁ ‖]

977

EN My friends arrived on Friday.

FR Mes amis (♀amies) sont arrivés (♀arrivées) vendredi.
IPA [me z‿ami (♀ami) sɔ̃ aʁive (♀aʁive) vɑ̃dʁᵊdi ‖]

978

EN Keiko went out at five [o'clock] (5:00).

FR Keiko est sorti à dix-sept heures (17 h).
IPA [(...) e sɔʁti a disɛ t‿œʁ (17 h) ‖]

979

EN I wore my new suit yesterday.

FR J'ai porté mon nouvel habit hier.
IPA [ʒ‿ɛ pɔʁte mɔ̃ nuvɛ l‿abi jɛʁ ‖]

980

EN Have you seen Veda? > Did you see Veda yesterday?

FR As-tu vu Veda? As-tu vu Veda hier soir?

IPA [a ty vy (...) || a ty vy (...) jɛʁ swaʁ ||]

981

EN I've finished my work. > I finished my work at two [o'clock] (2:00).

FR J'ai fini mon travail. J'ai fini mon travail à quatorze heures (14 h).

IPA [ʒ‿ɛ fini mɔ̃ tʁavaj || ʒ‿ɛ fini mɔ̃ tʁavaj a katɔʁz œʁ (14 h) ||]

982

EN Have you finished? > What time did you finish your work?

FR As-tu fini? À quelle heure as-tu fini ton travail?

IPA [a ty fini || a kɛ l‿œʁ a ty fini tɔ̃ tʁavaj ||]

983

EN Liting isn't here; she's gone out.

FR Liting n'est pas ici, elle est sortie.

IPA [(...) n‿e pa z‿isi | ɛ l‿e sɔʁti ||]

984

EN Sanjit's grandmother has died. > Sanjit's grandmother died two (2) years ago.

FR La grand-mère de Sanjit est morte. La grand-mère de Sanjit est morte il y a deux ans.

IPA [la gʁɑ̃mɛʁ dø (...) e mɔʁt ‖ la gʁɑ̃mɛʁ dø (...) e mɔʁt i l̩ i a dø z‿ɑ̃ ‖]

985

EN Where have you been? > Where were you last night?

FR Où étais-tu? Où étais-tu hier soir?

IPA [u etɛ ty ‖ u etɛ ty jɛʁ swaʁ ‖]

986

EN My friend is a writer, and has written many books.

FR Mon ami est un écrivain et il a écrit plusieurs livres.

IPA [mɔ̃ n‿ami e t‿œ̃ n‿ekʁivɛ̃ e i l̩a ekʁi plyzjœʁ livʁ ‖]

987

EN I played tennis yesterday afternoon.

FR J'ai joué au tennis hier après-midi.

IPA [ʒ‿ɛ ʒwe o tenis jɛ apʁɛ midi ‖]

988

EN What time did you go to bed last night?

FR À quelle heure es-tu allé au lit hier soir?
IPA [a kɛ l‿œʁ ɛ ty ale o li jɛʁ swaʁ ‖]

989

EN Have you ever met a famous person?

FR As-tu déjà rencontré une célébrité?
IPA [a ty deʒa ʁɑ̃kɔ̃tʁe yn selebʁite ‖]

990

EN The weather wasn't very good yesterday.

FR Le temps n'était pas très beau hier.
IPA [lø tɑ̃ n‿etɛ pa tʁɛ bo jɛʁ ‖]

991

EN Mira travels a lot. She's visited many countries.

FR Mira voyage beaucoup. Elle a visité plusieurs pays.
IPA [(...) vwajaʒ boku ‖ ɛ l‿a vizite plyzjœʁ pei ‖]

992

EN I turned off the light before leaving this morning.

FR J'ai fermé la lumière avant de partir ce matin.
IPA [ʒ‿ɛ fɛʁme la lymjɛʁ avɑ̃ dø paʁtiʁ sø matɛ̃ ‖]

993

EN I live in New York now, but I've lived in Mexico for many years.

FR Je vis à New York maintenant, mais j'ai vécu au Mexique durant plusieurs années.

IPA [ʒø vis a nuw jɔʁk mɛ̃t°nã | mɛ ʒ‿ɛ veky o meksik dyʁã plyzjœ ʁ‿ane ||]

994

EN What's Taiwan like? Is it beautiful? — I don't know. I've never been there.

FR Comment est Taïwan? C'est beau? — Je ne sais pas. Je n'y suis jamais allé.

IPA [komã t‿e taiwan || sɛ bo || — ʒø nø sɛ pa || ʒø n‿i sɥi ʒamɛ z‿ale ||]

995

EN Have you ever been to Florida?

FR Es-tu déjà allé (♀allée) en Floride?

IPA [ɛ ty deʒa ale (♀ale) ã floʁid ||]

996

EN We went there on vacation two (2) years ago.

FR Nous sommes allés (♀allées) en vacances là-bas il y a deux ans.

IPA [nu sɔm ale (♀ale) ã vakãs laba z‿i l‿i a dø z‿ã ||]

997

EN Did you have a good time?

FR As-tu passé du bon temps?
IPA [a ty pase dy bɔ̃ tɑ̃ ||]

998

EN We had a great time. It was wonderful.

FR Nous avons eu du bon temps. C'était merveilleux.
IPA [nu z‿avɔ̃ y dy bɔ̃ tɑ̃ || se etɛ mɛʁvɛjø ||]

999

EN What does your girlfriend do?

FR Qu'est-ce que ta copine fait?
IPA [kɛsᵊ kø ta kopin fɛ ||]

1000

EN She's a painter. She's won many prizes for her paintings.

FR Elle est peintre. Elle a gagné plusieurs prix pour ses tableaux.
IPA [ɛ l‿e pɛ̃tʁ || ɛ l‿a gaɲe plyzjœʁ pʁi puʁ se tablo ||]

French Index

a   [a]: 68, 279, 419, 482, 483, 490, 491, 496, 497, 498, 499, 500, 501, 527, 556, 570, 571, 574... +52

à   [a]: 7, 8, 17, 29, 30, 44, 54, 55, 56, 57, 58, 63, 79, 110, 117, 174, 219, 263, 264... +142

a   [l_a]: 13, 69, 150, 285, 360, 479, 484, 501, 505, 508, 517, 525, 571, 580, 583, 594, 595, 596, 598, 600... +22

a   [n_a]: 497, 500, 511, 539, 573, 576

a   [z_a]: 601

acheté   [aʃºte]: 588, 602, 631, 658, 885, 899, 906, 910, 911, 912, 934, 953, 966

acheté   [z_aʃºte]: 900

actuellement   [aktɥɛlºmã]: 529, 665

adore   [adɔʁ]: 769

adresse   [l_adʁɛs]: 950

affaires   [ʁ_afɛʁ]: 395, 395

âge   [l_aʒ]: 23, 49, 68, 123, 137, 149

ai   [ɛ]: 494, 495, 900, 933

ai   [ʁ_ɛ]: 914, 914

ai   [z_ɛ]: 715, 811

aime   [ɛm]: 403

aimé   [eme]: 572, 584, 624

aime   [l_ɛm]: 260, 307, 356, 850

aimé   [z_eme]: 613, 657

aiment   [ɛm]: 306, 344, 350, 357, 361, 485, 516

aiment-ils   [ɛ m_il]: 384

aimes-tu   [ɛm ty]: 389, 402, 761

aime-t-il   [ɛm t_il]: 385

alaska   [alaska]: 774

allait   [l_alɛ]: 723

allé   [ale]: 599, 632, 643, 644, 725, 773, 784, 786, 790, 797, 812, 879, 881, 901, 971, 988, 995

allé   [z_ale]: 773, 812, 994

allée   [ale]: 643, 644, 725, 779, 784, 786, 790, 797, 812, 879, 881, 971, 995

allée   [t_ale]: 577, 793, 794, 898

allée   [z_ale]: 730

allées   [ale]: 603, 613, 620, 633, 651, 657, 774, 963, 996

aller   [ale]: 361, 521

aller   [z_ale]: 355, 947, 949

allés   [ale]: 603, 613, 620, 633, 651, 657, 774, 996

allés   [z_ale]: 620, 774, 963

allons   [z_alɔ̃]: 291, 603

alors   [alɔ]: 539, 949

alors   [alɔʁ]: 559, 579, 660, 661, 670, 718, 728, 734, 771

américaine   [t_ameʁikɛn]: 97

ami   [n_ami]: 5, 86, 958, 972, 986

amie   [ami]: 972

amie   [n_ami]: 78, 957, 959

amies   [ami]: 361, 375, 601, 606, 635, 721, 847, 848, 924, 939, 977

amies   [z_ami]: 392

amis   [ami]: 847, 848

amis   [z_ami]: 219, 302, 361, 375, 392, 601, 606, 635, 721, 924, 939, 977

an   [n_ã]: 881

anglais   [ãglɛ]: 386, 393, 460

anglais   [n_ãglɛ]: 268, 269

animaux   [z_animo]: 485, 516

année   [ʁ_ane]: 762

années   [k_ane]: 750, 763, 770

années   [ʁ_ane]: 875, 912, 993

annoncé   [anɔ̃se]: 924

ans   [ã]: 69, 871

ans   [k_ã]: 50, 820, 836

ans   [t_ã]: 13, 24, 866, 882, 883, 894

ans   [z_ã]: 124, 138, 150, 539, 585, 829, 845, 862, 893, 974, 984, 996

appartement   [n_apaʁtºmã]: 741

appel [n̩_apɛl]: 410
appelé [ap°le]: 662, 710, 940
appelée [ap°le]: 710
appeler [z_ap°le]: 914
après [apʁɛ]: 541
après-midi [apʁɛ midi]: 582, 639, 962, 987
arrêté [aʁete]: 724, 731, 763
arrêtée [aʁete]: 731
arrive [aʁiv]: 244
arrivé [aʁive]: 637, 638, 727, 938, 973
arrive [l_aʁiv]: 277, 303
arrivé [t_aʁive]: 597, 718, 720, 728, 884
arrivé [z_aʁive]: 970, 973
arrivée [aʁive]: 637, 867
arrivée [t_aʁive]: 595, 816, 868
arrivées [aʁive]: 977
arrivés [aʁive]: 929, 932, 935, 977
arrive-t-il [aʁiv t_il]: 938
as [a]: 493
assis [asi]: 192, 253, 473, 578
assise [t_asiz]: 174, 184
as-tu [a ty]: 23, 49, 84, 104, 137, 152, 443, 494, 495, 510, 514, 612, 614, 623, 624, 625, 626, 627, 640, 649... +32
a-t-elle [a t_ɛl]: 149, 491, 492, 496, 841
a-t-il [a t_il]: 490, 513, 554, 615, 659, 777, 842
attend [l_atɑ̃]: 170
attendaient [atɑ̃dɛ]: 715
attendait [atɑ̃dɛ]: 680
attendons [z_atɑ̃dɔ̃]: 859, 935
attends [atɑ̃]: 231
attends-tu [atɑ̃ ty]: 211, 212
attendu [atɑ̃dy]: 596
attentons [attentons]: 860
au [o]: 11, 17, 115, 122, 166, 171, 180, 276, 277, 279, 280, 290, 291, 304, 313, 315, 357, 361, 376, 388... +80
aujourd'hui [oʒuʁdɥi]: 1, 15, 31, 32, 33, 34, 113, 153, 215, 549, 559, 583, 672, 729, 816, 856, 969, 973
aujourd'hui [z_oʒuʁdɥi]: 216

australie [ostʁali]: 779, 871
australien [ostʁaljɛ̃]: 135
autobus [n̩_otobys]: 315, 316, 451, 452, 791, 814
autour [otuʁ]: 273
autour [t_otuʁ]: 804
aux [o]: 296
aux [z_o]: 38
avais [avɛ]: 765
avait [avɛ]: 539, 750
avait [l_avɛ]: 621
avait [z_avɛ]: 747
avance [n̩_avɑ̃s]: 16
avant [avɑ̃]: 629, 632, 747, 752, 992
avant [t_avɑ̃]: 314
avec [avɛk]: 475, 591
avez-vous [ave vu]: 634
avion [n̩_avjɔ̃]: 781, 814
avions [z_avjɔ̃]: 541, 749
avoir [avwaʁ]: 550
avons [z_avɔ̃]: 511, 572, 573, 576, 584, 635, 707, 770, 899, 906, 910, 911, 912, 955, 974, 998
avril [z_avʁil]: 827, 846
bain [bɛ̃]: 79
balle [bal]: 735
banque [bɑ̃k]: 262, 570, 620, 836
banques [bɑ̃k]: 294, 559
bars [baʁ]: 355
baseball [bezbol]: 348, 733, 735, 753
bateau [bato]: 814
bâtiment [batimɑ̃]: 757
beau [bo]: 1, 165, 324, 536, 543, 549, 568, 617, 652, 653, 659, 737, 990, 994
beaucoup [boku]: 258, 265, 274, 289, 297, 299, 300, 326, 327, 331, 363, 364, 369, 370, 372, 415, 432, 485, 509... +19
beaux [bo]: 311
bel [bɛ]: 584
belle [bɛl]: 372, 488, 523, 583
belles [bɛl]: 14, 625, 642
besoin [bøzwɛ̃]: 443, 914

bien [bjɛ̃]: 71, 81, 107, 120, 200, 201, 255, 256, 269, 302, 336, 338, 339, 420, 435, 484, 522, 551, 627... +5

billet [bijɛ]: 521

billets [bijɛ]: 588

bleu [blø]: 28

bleue [blø]: 94

bleus [blø]: 481

bois [bwa]: 317, 320

boit [bwa]: 318, 321, 370

bon [bɔ̃]: 37, 43, 74, 268, 467, 657, 997, 998

bonne [bɔn]: 924

bons [bɔ̃]: 6, 302

bord [bɔʁ]: 788, 796

bout [bu]: 301

boxe [bɔks]: 347

bras [bʁa]: 717, 915

brésil [bʁezil]: 36, 777, 815, 816, 817, 818, 819, 839, 855, 867, 869, 870, 888

breuvage [bʁœvaʒ]: 370

brillait [bʁijɛ]: 674

brille [bʁij]: 197, 218

brille-t-il [bʁij t_il]: 217

brosse [bʁɔs]: 569

brossé [bʁose]: 569, 947

bu [by]: 593

bureau [byʁo]: 116, 261, 620, 872, 950

bus [bys]: 121, 170, 231

ça [sa]: 275, 363, 364, 440, 646, 647, 663, 762

cadeau [kado]: 900

café [kafe]: 317, 318, 320, 321, 370, 480, 593, 596

caméra [kameʁa]: 92, 490, 494, 495, 566

camion [kamjɔ̃]: 799

campagne [kɑ̃paɲ]: 755

canada [kanada]: 65, 388, 466, 774, 846, 857, 858

canadien [kanadjɛ̃]: 136

cartes [kaʁt]: 72

cassé [kase]: 717, 735, 792, 915

cassée [kase]: 230, 654, 655, 656

ce [sø]: 3, 34, 88, 89, 91, 371, 379, 407, 422, 423, 426, 439, 450, 453, 456, 545, 551, 563, 569... +18

célèbre [selebʁ]: 396

célébrité [selebʁite]: 989

célibataire [selibatɛʁ]: 48

cent [sɑ̃]: 301, 688, 833, 866, 873

centre-ville [sɑ̃tʁ°vil]: 180, 598, 770

cents [sɑ̃]: 566, 570

certain [sɛʁtɛ̃]: 732

certaine [sɛʁtɛn]: 732

ces [se]: 4, 14, 72, 125, 553, 746, 749, 875, 885

cessé [sese]: 571, 704

c'est [sɛ]: 33, 77, 90, 109, 130, 228, 367, 369, 370, 372, 467, 488, 523, 583, 718, 900, 994

cet [sɛ]: 74, 76, 364, 776, 783

cet [sɛt]: 639

c'était [se etɛ]: 568, 673, 998

cette [sɛt]: 108, 129, 555, 577, 807, 852

chaise [ʃɛz]: 192

chaises [ʃɛz]: 14

chambre [ʃɑ̃bʁ]: 59, 557, 718

champignons [ʃɑ̃piɲɔ̃]: 751

chantaient [ʃɑ̃tɛ]: 674

chante [ʃɑ̃t]: 470

chapeau [ʃapo]: 188, 699

chaque [ʃak]: 476

chats [ʃa]: 485, 516

chaud [ʃo]: 15, 31, 32, 579, 661

chauffeur [ʃofœʁ]: 9, 754

chaussures [ʃosyʁ]: 61, 131, 198, 300, 544, 553, 885

chemises [ʃ°miz]: 658

cher [ʃɛʁ]: 74, 275, 299, 300, 364, 542, 544, 553, 554

cheval [ʃ°val]: 485, 782

cheveux [ʃ°vø]: 190, 378, 747

chez [ʃe]: 220, 365, 635, 695

chien [ʃjɛ̃]: 498, 503

chiens [ʃjɛ̃]: 485, 516, 540

chinois [ʃinwa]: 86

chocolat [ʃokola]: 306, 389, 389, 745

chose [ʃoz]: 249, 343, 478, 519, 550

choses [ʃoz]: 274, 803

cinéma [sinema]: 291, 304, 361, 406, 577, 603, 613, 657, 879

cinq [sɛ̃]: 820, 836

cinq [sɛ̃k]: 124, 878, 909

circulation [siʁkylasjɔ̃]: 122, 563

classique [klasik]: 344

clé [kle]: 507, 526, 740, 904

clés [kle]: 88, 561, 600, 907, 908, 909

combien [kɔ̃bjɛ̃]: 72, 125, 380, 410, 466, 514, 566, 646, 777, 824, 826, 828, 830, 841, 842

comme [kɔm]: 463

commence [komɑ̃s]: 271, 771, 936

commencé [komɑ̃se]: 580, 713, 863, 936, 942, 943, 957, 976

commence-t-elle [komɑ̃s t_ɛl]: 942

comment [komɑ̃]: 19, 45, 70, 80, 106, 111, 119, 133, 655, 656, 663, 741, 994

complet [kɔ̃plɛ]: 692

comprends [kɔ̃pʁɑ̃]: 438, 474

compte [kɔ̃t]: 925, 959

concert [kɔ̃sɛʁ]: 521

conduire [kɔ̃dɥiʁ]: 451

conduisais [kɔ̃dɥizɛ]: 732

conduisais-tu [kɔ̃dɥizɛ ty]: 731

conduisait [kɔ̃dɥizɛ]: 679

conduisait-elle [kɔ̃dɥizɛ t_ɛl]: 691

conduit [kɔ̃dɥi]: 594, 791, 799

conduit-elle [kɔ̃dɥi t_ɛl]: 452

confortable [kɔ̃fɔʁtabl]: 542

confortables [kɔ̃fɔʁtabl]: 14

connais [konɛ]: 363, 823, 847, 848, 891

connaissent [konɛs]: 326, 340

connais-tu [konɛ ty]: 822, 840, 887

connaît-elle [konɛ t_ɛl]: 810

consomme [kɔ̃sɔm]: 331

construisent [kɔ̃stʁɥi]: 180

copié [kopje]: 589

copine [kopin]: 999

corée [koʁe]: 786

couché [kuʃe]: 172

coucher [kuʃe]: 898

couleur [kulœʁ]: 27, 28, 66, 102, 131

coupe [kup]: 777

coupé [kupe]: 663

couple [kupl]: 681

courant [kuʁɑ̃]: 664

courriel [kuʁjɛl]: 914, 970, 973

courrier [kuʁje]: 727

course [kuʁs]: 789

courses [kuʁs]: 678, 795, 922

courts [kuʁ]: 747

coûtait [kutɛ]: 542

coûte [kut]: 275, 299, 364, 380, 410, 466

coûté [kute]: 544, 554, 646, 647

coûtent [kut]: 125, 300, 553

crois [kʁwa]: 371, 446

crois-tu [kʁwa ty]: 445

cuisine [kɥizin]: 175, 242, 478, 687

cuisiner [kɥizine]: 478

d'action [d_aksjɔ̃]: 351

d'amis [d_ami]: 327, 525

d'animaux [d_animo]: 485

d'anneau [d_ano]: 362

dans [dɑ̃]: 59, 93, 175, 177, 178, 261, 262, 274, 288, 355, 404, 413, 473, 478, 493, 519, 570, 578, 579... +19

danse [dɑ̃s]: 284

dansé [dɑ̃se]: 573

d'appeler [d_apᵊle]: 940

d'argent [d_aʁʒɑ̃]: 299, 300, 364, 509, 514

d'arriver [d_aʁive]: 926

date [dat]: 555

d'autobus [d_otobys]: 715

de [də]: 6, 9, 22, 66, 75, 79, 96, 101, 102, 116, 121, 122, 131, 146, 157, 158, 159, 163... +137

décollé [dekole]: 597

d'écrire [d_ekʁiʁ]: 189

degrés [dᵊgʁe]: 301

déjà [deʒa]: 586, 760, 773, 776, 778, 779, 780, 784, 785, 786, 787, 788, 789, 790, 791, 792, 795, 797, 800, 807... +25

déjeune [deʒœn]: 266

déjeuné [deʒœne]: 969, 975
déjeuner [deʒœne]: 173, 337, 411, 571, 596, 685, 686, 728
déjeunes-tu [deʒœn ty]: 381
d'électricité [d_elɛktʁisite]: 925
demain [dᵊmɛ̃]: 224, 900
demande [dᵊmɑ̃d]: 497, 498, 499, 500, 501
demande-lui [dᵊmɑ̃d lɥi]: 957, 958, 959, 960
demander [dᵊmɑ̃de]: 923
déménagé [demenaʒe]: 770, 916
d'enfants [d_ɑ̃fɑ̃]: 487
d'enseigner [d_ɑ̃seɲe]: 457
dentiste [dɑ̃tist]: 463, 695
dents [dɑ̃]: 569, 947
dépêche-toi [depɛʃ twa]: 528
dépend [depɑ̃]: 440
depuis [dᵊpɥi]: 817, 818, 819, 820, 821, 822, 823, 824, 826, 827, 828, 829, 830, 831, 833, 834, 835, 836, 837, 838... +38
dernier [dɛʁnje]: 539, 552, 555, 582, 584, 592, 603, 606, 633, 876, 963, 971
dernière [dɛʁnjɛʁ]: 536, 558, 565, 568, 587, 600, 717, 740, 877, 878, 879, 880, 881, 908, 911, 976
dernières [dɛʁnjɛ]: 912
des [de]: 308, 361, 448, 454, 501, 524, 540, 635, 756, 803, 806, 811
descendue [desɑ̃dy]: 720
désolé [dezole]: 176, 368, 473, 474, 849
d'essence [d_esɑ̃s]: 331
d'étudier [d_etydje]: 195
deux [dø]: 126, 482, 501, 506, 516, 566, 570, 602, 658, 671, 721, 738, 778, 790, 793, 812, 829, 851, 859... +5
devenir [dᵊvᵊniʁ]: 581
devoirs [dᵊvwaʁ]: 163, 612, 946
devrais-je [dᵊvʁɛ ʒø]: 902
d'habitude [d_abityd]: 383
d'horreur [d_oʁœʁ]: 350
d'hôtel [d_otɛl]: 766

diamants [djamɑ̃]: 37
d'ici [d_isi]: 116, 375, 391
différente [difeʁɑ̃t]: 866
différentes [difeʁɑ̃t]: 274
différents [difeʁɑ̃]: 775, 801
difficile [difisil]: 564
dimanche [dimɑ̃ʃ]: 279, 538, 582, 603, 615, 962
dimanches [dimɑ̃ʃ]: 374
dîné [dine]: 865
dîner [dine]: 167, 182, 401, 927, 945
dînons [dinɔ̃]: 161, 310
dire [diʁ]: 444
discuté [diskyte]: 591
dit [di]: 669, 933, 954
dix [di]: 124, 675, 683, 706, 707, 845, 862
dix [dis]: 685, 802, 864
dix-huit [dizɥi]: 310, 665
dix-neuf [diznœ]: 580
dix-sept [disɛ]: 295, 430, 831, 978
d'octobre [d_ɔktɔbʁ]: 876
doit [dwa]: 959
donc [dɔ̃k]: 713
donné [done]: 950
d'ordinateur [d_ɔʁdinatœʁ]: 502
dormais [dɔʁmɛ]: 739
dormait [dɔʁmɛ]: 532
dormi [dɔʁmi]: 627, 649, 650
dort [dɔʁ]: 292
d'où [d_u]: 21, 64, 100, 114, 145, 465
douche [duʃ]: 179, 426, 431, 468, 605, 630
drôle [dʁol]: 228, 462
du [dy]: 65, 186, 273, 287, 294, 317, 320, 321, 338, 339, 394, 416, 571, 738, 758, 767, 777, 786... +5
d'un [d_œ̃]: 466, 760, 788, 796
dur [dyʁ]: 305
durant [dyʁɑ̃]: 312, 893, 993
d'y [d_i]: 364
écrit [ekʁi]: 802, 803, 809, 914, 965, 972, 986
écrivain [n_ekʁivɛ̃]: 965, 986

elle   [d_ɛ]: 595
elle   [ɛ]: 17, 56, 67, 79, 93, 95, 97, 144,
       150, 174, 184, 230, 277, 285, 296,
       303, 307, 356, 362... +42
elle   [ɛl]: 17, 101, 146, 148, 159, 169,
       179, 182, 183, 185, 263, 276, 281,
       283, 286, 289, 293, 299, 302, 305...
       +54
elle   [ʁ_ɛ]: 539
elle   [ʁ_ɛl]: 672, 900, 949
elle   [t_ɛl]: 656
elles [ɛ]: 561
elles [ɛl]: 14, 62, 73, 132, 154, 171,
       288, 300, 326, 327, 340, 344, 347,
       350, 357, 361, 384, 392, 457, 458...
       +33
emplois [ʁ_ãplwa]: 775, 801
en   [ã]: 16, 53, 98, 118, 167, 178, 315,
     316, 422, 423, 426, 449, 450, 451,
     453, 455, 456, 478, 479... +35
en   [l_ã]: 497, 500, 539
en   [p_ã]: 265, 432
en   [ʁ_ã]: 358, 814
en   [t_ã]: 158, 163, 249, 457, 565, 815,
     871, 874, 901
en   [z_ã]: 16, 157, 159, 182, 186, 189,
     190, 193, 195, 199, 332, 537, 543,
     567, 711, 767, 815, 849
encore   [ãkɔʁ]: 923
encore   [z_ãkɔʁ]: 900, 925, 932, 933,
       934, 935, 947, 951, 973
endormi   [ãdɔʁmi]: 533
endormie [ãdɔʁmi]: 716
endroit   [l_ãdʁwa]: 405, 584
endroits [ʁ_ãdʁwa]: 775
enfant   [n_ãfã]: 540, 581, 745, 751, 768,
       772
enfants [z_ãfã]: 8, 117, 119, 123, 163,
       166, 208, 296, 306, 506, 556
enlevé   [ãl°ve]: 578
ennuyant   [z_ãnɥijã]: 367
enregistrée   [ãʁ°ʒistʁe]: 595
enseignant   [ãsɛɲã]: 26, 139, 156, 843
enseignante   [ãsɛɲãt]: 26, 139, 156
enseignante   [t_ãsɛɲãt]: 144, 296
enseigne   [l_ãsɛɲ]: 296

enseignent-ils   [ãsɛɲ t_il]: 458
ensoleillé   [ãsoleje]: 15
ensuite   [ãsɥit]: 596
entendu   [ãtãdy]: 920
entré   [ãtʁe]: 578, 741
équipe   [n_ekip]: 733
erreur   [ɛʁœʁ]: 917
es   [ɛ]: 16, 54, 725
escaladé   [ɛskalade]: 742
espagne   [espagne]: 793, 971
espagnol   [ɛspaɲɔl]: 335
essayait   [esejɛ]: 960
est   [e]: 3, 7, 10, 28, 36, 63, 66, 76, 78,
     92, 102, 108, 121, 128, 129, 158,
     179, 297, 298, 461... +47
est   [l_e]: 7, 11, 13, 17, 25, 27, 43, 56,
     67, 75, 79, 93, 95, 97, 103, 127,
     144, 147, 172... +46
est   [n_e]: 651
est   [t_e]: 994
est   [z_e]: 268
est-ce   [ɛs°]: 202, 215, 244, 251, 255,
       375, 376, 382, 386, 387, 388, 403,
       415, 438, 442, 457, 490, 491, 560,
       564... +18
est-elle   [e t_ɛl]: 55, 63, 94, 96, 110,
       143, 451, 779, 817, 867, 869
est-il   [e t_il]: 74, 86, 112, 116, 368,
       449, 455, 727, 864, 901, 967
es-tu   [ɛ ty]: 47, 51, 82, 118, 135, 139,
       141, 151, 156, 253, 429, 637, 643,
       741, 773, 784, 786, 790, 821... +7
et   [e]: 6, 15, 124, 272, 389, 390, 394,
     396, 420, 485, 501, 505, 516, 557,
     560, 573, 578, 580... +44
et   [n_e]: 302, 900
et   [z_e]: 330
étaient   [etɛ]: 548, 556, 559, 560, 565
étaient   [l_etɛ]: 561
étaient-ils   [etɛ t_il]: 548, 565
étais   [etɛ]: 537, 543, 567, 772
étais-tu   [etɛ ty]: 545, 546, 552, 562,
       563, 567, 962, 985
était   [etɛ]: 535, 542, 547, 557, 558,
       560, 563, 564, 580, 679, 680, 725,
       729, 757, 766, 866, 965

était [l_etɛ]: 531, 533, 564, 566, 666, 730, 754

était [n_etɛ]: 566

était [ʁ_etɛ]: 559

était-il [etɛ t_il]: 547

états-unis [z_etazuni]: 38

été [ete]: 800, 805, 878, 880

éteindre [etɛ̃dʁ]: 428, 477

êtes [z_ɛt]: 473

étions [z_etjɔ̃]: 660, 711

être [ɛtʁ]: 396

étudiait [l_etydjɛ]: 726

étudiant [etydjɑ̃]: 51

étudiante [etydjɑ̃t]: 51

étudie [etydi]: 886

étudié [etydje]: 841, 893

étudies-tu [etydi ty]: 828

eu [y]: 625, 642, 775, 801, 998

eu [z_y]: 612, 662

euro [n_øʁo]: 73

euros [øʁo]: 647

euros [z_øʁo]: 126, 566

eux [ø]: 392

examen [n_ɛgzamɛ̃]: 564

excusez-moi [ɛkskyze mwa]: 473

fâché [faʃe]: 567

fâchée [faʃe]: 567

facile [fasil]: 564

facteur [faktœʁ]: 951

faim [fɛ̃]: 12, 41, 42, 84, 104, 105, 541, 550, 927, 945

faire [fɛʁ]: 163, 511

fais [fɛ]: 343, 394, 429

faisaient [fᵊzɛ]: 678

faisais-tu [fᵊzɛ ty]: 668, 677, 689, 706, 738

faisait [fᵊzɛ]: 536, 549, 579, 652, 653, 661, 681, 701, 734

faisait-il [fᵊzɛ t_il]: 543, 568

faisons [fᵊzɔ̃]: 274, 278

fais-tu [fɛ ty]: 383, 394, 404, 434, 758

fait [fɛ]: 1, 15, 31, 32, 153, 155, 205, 324, 336, 463, 612, 617, 659, 663, 703, 705, 917, 922, 955... +2

fait-elle [fɛ t_ɛl]: 453

fait-il [fɛ t_il]: 59, 153, 155, 206, 450, 456

fatigué [fatige]: 39, 40, 82, 534, 551, 648, 660

fatiguée [fatige]: 39, 40, 82, 471, 534, 551, 648

fatiguées [fatige]: 660

fatigués [fatige]: 541

faut [fo]: 165

favori [favoʁi]: 127, 128, 370

femme [fam]: 108, 143, 807, 916

fenêtre [fᵊnetʁ]: 579, 654, 661, 742

férié [feʁje]: 559

ferme [fɛʁm]: 295

fermé [fɛʁme]: 992

fermées [fɛʁme]: 559

fête [fɛt]: 548, 560, 572, 574, 616, 624, 660, 915

fêtes [fɛt]: 307

feu [fø]: 122

film [film]: 227, 580, 613, 657, 813, 939

films [film]: 350, 351, 352, 361

finalement [finalᵊmɑ̃]: 598

fini [fini]: 574, 580, 626, 713, 946, 981, 982

finit [fini]: 272, 286

finit-il [fini t_il]: 476

floride [floʁid]: 995

fois [fwa]: 577, 762, 777, 778, 779, 789, 790, 792, 793, 794, 797, 800, 805, 808, 812, 813, 877, 878, 879, 880... +2

fonctionne-t-elle [fɔ̃ksjɔn t_ɛl]: 229

font [fɔ̃]: 208

font-ils [fɔ̃ t_il]: 459

foot [fut]: 171

football [futbɔl]: 328, 329, 402, 403

fort [fɔʁ]: 270, 322, 341, 387, 397

france [fʁɑ̃s]: 773

frappé [fʁape]: 735

fréquence [fʁekɑ̃s]: 378, 400, 408, 472

frère [fʁɛʁ]: 6, 262, 393, 403, 501, 812, 902, 916

frères [fʁɛʁ]: 501, 505
froid [fʁwa]: 59, 153, 205, 549
froides [fʁwad]: 35, 154
fruits [fʁɥi]: 289
gagné [gaɲe]: 611, 640, 733, 777, 789, 795, 1000
garage [gaʁaʒ]: 488
gare [gaʁ]: 680, 720, 723
garé [gaʁe]: 595
généralement [ʒeneʁal°mã]: 294, 306, 310, 312, 316, 324, 337, 361, 409, 411, 434, 479, 575, 602
gens [ʒã]: 297, 308, 326, 573, 806
gérant [ʒeʁã]: 766
glace [glas]: 259, 260, 696
golf [gɔlf]: 780, 785
grand [gʁã]: 36, 523
grand-chose [gʁãʃoz]: 363
grande [gʁãd]: 288, 413
grandes [gʁãd]: 267
grand-mère [gʁãmɛʁ]: 984
grand-père [gʁãpɛʁ]: 585
grasse [gʁas]: 278
gros [gʁo]: 945
guitare [gitaʁ]: 418, 419, 420, 421, 422, 423, 424, 760
gym [ʒim]: 666
habit [l̯abi]: 979
habitaient [abitɛ]: 748, 755
habitais-tu [abitɛ ty]: 688, 752
habite [abit]: 388
habite [l̯abit]: 365, 391
habitent [abit]: 264
habitent-ils [abi t̯il]: 398
habites [abit]: 391, 415
hais [ɛ]: 442
hélicoptère [elikɔptɛʁ]: 788, 796
heure [l̯œʁ]: 409, 476, 637, 727, 929, 938, 941, 967, 982, 988
heure [œʁ]: 865, 884, 890, 975
heures [œʁ]: 552, 597, 666, 668, 677, 689, 707, 713, 930, 981
heures [t̯œʁ]: 271, 272, 292, 295, 310, 314, 430, 594, 629, 665, 682, 684, 686, 771, 831, 872, 978

heures [v̯œʁ]: 294, 430, 575, 580, 638, 687, 713, 860
heures [z̯œʁ]: 580, 593, 632, 675, 683, 706, 707, 738, 851, 859, 877
heureux [z̯øʁø]: 517
hier [jɛ]: 559, 672, 987
hier [jɛʁ]: 530, 534, 535, 537, 547, 549, 551, 562, 567, 571, 572, 576, 576, 583, 591, 599, 601, 602, 604, 608... +30
hier [t̯jɛʁ]: 673
hiver [n̯ivɛʁ]: 265, 432
homme [l̯ɔm]: 13
homme [t̯ɔm]: 76, 776, 783
hôtel [l̯otɛl]: 180
hôtel [n̯otɛl]: 178, 598, 757, 850
hôtel [t̯otɛl]: 74, 364
huit [ɥi]: 682, 684
huit [ɥit]: 873
ici [isi]: 408, 752, 889, 905, 926, 928, 932
ici [s̯isi]: 916
ici [z̯isi]: 538, 913, 983
il [i]: 7, 11, 13, 43, 69, 103, 170, 172, 175, 249, 260, 332, 360, 365, 373, 391, 475, 478... +59
il [il]: 1, 15, 31, 32, 81, 87, 107, 153, 155, 165, 175, 186, 187, 188, 189, 191, 194, 205, 207... +75
il [ʁ̯i]: 763
il [z̯i]: 883, 996
ils [i]: 506, 617, 916
ils [il]: 58, 71, 120, 166, 171, 180, 209, 220, 257, 258, 288, 326, 327, 340, 344, 347, 350, 357, 361, 485... +30
indépendant [ɛ̃depãdã]: 873
infirmière [t̯ɛ̃fiʁmjɛʁ]: 10
insecte [n̯ɛ̃sɛkt]: 527
instrument [ɛ̃stʁymã]: 760
intelligent [ɛ̃teliʒã]: 499
intéressant [ɛ̃teʁesã]: 112
intéressant [z̯ɛ̃teʁesã]: 297
intéressante [ɛ̃teʁesãt]: 775
intéressantes [ɛ̃teʁesãt]: 803
intéressants [ɛ̃teʁesã]: 806

intérêts [z ɛ̃teʀɛ]: 29
italien [z italjɛ̃]: 335
j'achète [ʒ aʃɛt]: 602
j'ai [ʒ ɛ]: 12, 24, 41, 50, 85, 138, 152, 481, 486, 519, 522, 550, 579, 586, 588, 589, 590, 591, 602, 604... +46
j'aimais [ʒ ɛmɛ]: 745
j'aime [ʒ ɛm]: 267, 346, 349, 352, 389, 554
j'aimerais [ʒ ɛmᵊʀɛ]: 762
jamais [ʒamɛ]: 298, 304, 309, 313, 353, 358, 773, 774, 781, 782, 783, 784, 785, 786, 787, 788, 791, 796, 798, 799... +4
jambe [ʒɑ̃b]: 792
janvier [ʒɑ̃vje]: 858
japon [ʒapɔ̃]: 671, 794
jardin [ʒaʀdɛ̃]: 523, 622
j'attends [ʒ atɑ̃]: 232
j'avais [ʒ avɛ]: 540, 746, 758, 759, 761, 762
jazz [dʒaz]: 345
je [ʒø]: 2, 9, 12, 16, 20, 22, 26, 30, 39, 40, 42, 44, 46, 48, 52, 65, 83, 105, 134... +173
j'écoute [ʒ ekut]: 196
j'écris [ʒ ekʀi]: 903
j'écrivais [ʒ ekʀivɛ]: 903
j'en [ʒ ɑ̃]: 765, 768
j'étais [ʒ etɛ]: 534, 540, 551, 555, 581, 636, 713, 745, 751, 768
j'étudie [ʒ etydi]: 828, 838
jeudi [ʒødi]: 816
jeux [ʒø]: 772
jolie [ʒoli]: 937
jolies [ʒoli]: 61, 72, 544
jouais [ʒwɛ]: 763
jouais-tu [ʒwɛ ty]: 772
jouait [ʒwɛ]: 683, 753
j'oublie [ʒ ubli]: 308
joue [ʒu]: 287, 290, 338, 339, 376, 390, 392, 416, 418, 420, 421, 422, 423, 424, 467, 764, 780, 894
joué [ʒwe]: 611, 639, 707, 734, 760, 780, 785, 798, 808, 987
jouent [ʒu]: 166, 171
jouent-elles [ʒu t ɛl]: 392
jouent-ils [ʒu t il]: 392
jouer [ʒwe]: 186, 279, 763
joues-tu [ʒu ty]: 390, 416, 760
joue-t-il [ʒu t il]: 423, 424
joueur [ʒwœʀ]: 467
joueurs [ʒwœʀ]: 6
jouions [ʒujɔ̃]: 708, 735
jour [ʒuʀ]: 439, 476, 559, 814
journal [ʒuʀnal]: 158, 199, 207, 851
journaux [ʒuʀno]: 602
journée [ʒuʀne]: 583, 832
jours [ʒuʀ]: 266, 343, 356, 359, 430, 602, 604, 758, 819, 834, 854, 855, 868, 870, 885, 888
jours-ci [ʒuʀ si]: 746, 749
jupe [ʒyp]: 672
jusqu'à [ʒyska]: 594, 598
jusqu'au [ʒysko]: 595
juste [ʒyst]: 808, 927, 948
j'y [ʒ i]: 181, 767
kilo [kilo]: 126
kilomètre [kilomɛtʀ]: 956
l'a [l a]: 750, 810, 813, 934, 942
là [la]: 556, 835
la [la]: 7, 17, 30, 44, 55, 57, 63, 79, 92, 110, 157, 168, 174, 175, 177, 178, 183, 196, 209, 221... +161
là-bas [laba]: 595, 815, 825, 854, 855, 856, 996
l'accident [l aksidɑ̃]: 582, 944
l'aéroport [l aeʀopɔʀ]: 594, 596, 598, 770
l'ai [l ɛ]: 520, 587, 614, 765, 778, 783, 813, 827, 904, 940
l'aime [l ɛm]: 302, 330, 372, 525
l'aimes [l ɛm]: 435, 436
l'allemand [l alᵊmɑ̃]: 828, 829
l'an [l ɑ̃]: 539, 555, 584, 876, 963, 971
l'anglais [l ɑ̃glɛ]: 195, 838, 886
langues [lɑ̃g]: 293, 366
l'anniversaire [l anivɛʀsɛʀ]: 900
l'arrêt [l aʀɛ]: 121, 715
l'as-tu [l a ty]: 919, 937
l'attendaient [l atɑ̃dɛ]: 721

l'attendons [l̪atɑ̃dɔ̃]: 874
l'autobus [l̪otobys]: 244, 874
lavait [lavɛ]: 682
lave [lav]: 298, 334, 895
lavé [lave]: 895
laver [lave]: 190, 333, 455
laves-tu [lav ty]: 378
lave-t-il [lav t̪il]: 454
l'avion [l̪avjɔ̃]: 597
l'avons [l̪avɔ̃]: 657
le [lø]: 16, 28, 36, 52, 62, 77, 83, 116,
  126, 128, 142, 151, 154, 156, 158,
  160, 172, 173, 176... +71
l'eau [l̪o]: 301
l'échelle [l̪eʃɛl]: 719
l'école [l̪ekɔl]: 7, 8, 117, 316, 800
l'écoute [l̪ekut]: 477
lentement [lɑ̃t̪ᵊmɑ̃]: 474, 903
l'envoi [l̪ɑ̃vwa]: 466
l'es [l̪ɛ]: 99
les [le]: 37, 89, 113, 163, 166, 190,
  208, 266, 267, 278, 294, 296, 300,
  306, 307, 343, 350, 351, 352, 355...
  +45
l'est [l̪e]: 87, 91
l'étais [l̪etɛ]: 546
l'éteindre [l̪etɛ̃dʁ]: 222
lettre [lɛtʁ]: 189
leur [lœ]: 914
leurs [lœʁ]: 163, 257
lève [lɛv]: 314, 575, 771
levé [lᵊve]: 575, 629, 690, 712, 837
levée [lᵊve]: 593, 690
lèves-tu [lɛv ty]: 399
l'extérieur [l̪eksteʁjœʁ]: 56, 58
l'habitude [l̪abityd]: 279, 479, 746,
  749, 758, 759, 761, 762
l'heure [l̪œʁ]: 54, 571, 597
l'homme [l̪ɔm]: 129
l'hôpital [l̪opital]: 876, 949
l'horaire [l̪oʁɛʁ]: 589
l'horloge [l̪oʁlɔʒ]: 229
l'hôtel [l̪otɛl]: 219, 542, 557
libres [libʁ]: 274, 404

ligne [liɲ]: 588
lire [liʁ]: 158, 199, 704, 746, 761
lis [lis]: 233, 313, 359, 746
lisa [lisa]: 96
lisait [lizɛ]: 684, 702
lisant [lizɑ̃]: 716
lisent [liz]: 258, 518
lis-tu [lis ty]: 472
lit [li]: 11, 158, 185, 207, 281, 313,
  409, 531, 533, 632, 851, 898, 930,
  947, 988
l'italien [l̪italjɛ̃]: 841
livre [livʁ]: 185, 702, 778
livres [livʁ]: 257, 518, 746, 802, 811,
  972, 986
l'œil [l̪œj]: 519
londres [lɔ̃dʁᵊ]: 101
long [lɔ̃]: 580
longs [lɔ̃]: 747
longtemps [lɔ̃tɑ̃]: 660, 823, 835, 848,
  853, 861, 876, 887
l'ont [l̪ɔ̃]: 939
lorsque [lɔʁskᵊ]: 540, 543, 581, 703,
  772
lorsqu'elle [lɔʁsk ɛl]: 722
lourd [luʁ]: 3
lourds [luʁ]: 4
lu [ly]: 778
lucie [lusi]: 480
lui [lɥi]: 391, 393, 395, 591, 900, 933
lumière [lymjɛʁ]: 992
lundi [lœ̃di]: 619, 816, 818, 856
lunettes [lynɛt]: 756
l'université [l̪ynivɛʁsite]: 893, 903
lus [ly]: 811
l'utilise [l̪ytiliz]: 360
lycée [lise]: 809
ma [ma]: 10, 28, 109, 331, 740, 781,
  871, 937
maalik [malik]: 854
magasins [magazɛ̃]: 113
magazine [magazin]: 631
magnifique [maɲifik]: 568, 673
m'aime [m̪ɛm]: 302, 330

main [mɛ̃]: 663
mains [mɛ̃]: 35, 154
maintenant [mɛ̃t°nã]: 155, 181, 213,
    214, 223, 226, 471, 539, 558, 561,
    744, 747, 766, 768, 850, 859, 895,
    898, 899, 901... +3
mais [mɛ]: 12, 14, 85, 280, 320, 321,
    332, 335, 359, 360, 361, 362, 365,
    419, 422, 467, 486, 488, 521, 523...
    +40
maison [mɛzɔ̃]: 7, 17, 55, 57, 63, 110,
    266, 288, 361, 471, 475, 488, 523,
    562, 594, 622, 665, 666, 698, 852...
    +8
maisons [mɛzɔ̃]: 875
mal [mal]: 484, 522, 837
malade [malad]: 11, 558, 730, 834,
    876, 878
mange [mãʒ]: 169, 250, 259, 289, 373,
    604, 768
mangé [mãʒe]: 604, 877
mangeais [mãʒɛ]: 768
mangeait [mãʒɛ]: 696
manger [mãʒe]: 159, 193, 249, 357,
    550, 945
manges [mãʒ]: 235
manges-tu [mãʒ ty]: 411
manteau [mãto]: 18, 204, 578, 853
m'appelle [m apɛl]: 20, 46, 134
marchait [maʁʃɛ]: 722
marché [maʁʃe]: 37, 176, 595
marcher [maʁʃe]: 479
mardi [maʁdi]: 592, 619, 889
mariaient [maʁjɛ]: 954
marié [maʁje]: 47, 141, 151, 821, 921
mariée [maʁje]: 47, 141, 151, 362, 805,
    821
mariés [maʁje]: 820, 833, 845, 882,
    883, 892
m'as [m a]: 176
mathématiques [matematik]: 296
matin [matɛ̃]: 294, 317, 545, 551, 563,
    569, 575, 605, 648, 662, 663, 673,
    705, 715, 727, 738, 837, 880, 992
matinée [matine]: 278, 571
matins [matɛ̃]: 381, 394, 431, 569

m'attends-tu [m atã ty]: 849
mauvais [movɛ]: 734
mauvaise [movɛz]: 563
me [mø]: 190, 201, 243, 256, 314, 315,
    316, 438, 442, 445, 522, 551, 569,
    575, 629, 663, 673, 712... +6
m'écoutes [m ekut]: 162
m'écoutes-tu [m ekut ty]: 239
médecin [mɛdsɛ̃]: 140, 143, 581
médecine [mɛdsin]: 893
même [mɛm]: 343, 748
mercredi [mɛʁkʁ°di]: 856
mère [mɛʁ]: 7, 55, 63, 110
merveilleux [mɛʁvejø]: 998
mes [me]: 35, 198, 561, 588, 907, 908,
    909, 977
métier [metje]: 25
mexico [mɛksiko]: 146, 592, 597
mexique [meksik]: 410, 873, 993
midi [midi]: 685
miennes [mjɛn]: 89
mieux [mjø]: 558
mille [mil]: 570, 671, 688, 833, 873,
    891
m'intéresse [m ɛ̃teʁɛs]: 30, 44, 363
minuit [minɥi]: 574
minutes [minyt]: 556, 724, 864, 874
mis [mi]: 590
moi [mwa]: 6, 220, 475, 847, 848
mois [mwa]: 633, 838, 857, 876, 878,
    886, 892
mois-ci [mwa si]: 909
moment [momã]: 422, 423, 426, 450,
    453, 456, 815, 854, 896, 897
mon [mɔ̃]: 5, 6, 90, 128, 130, 262, 297,
    340, 367, 473, 520, 590, 626, 812,
    897, 902, 916, 918, 923... +7
monde [mɔ̃d]: 525, 777, 804
montagnes [mɔ̃taɲ]: 644
monté [mɔ̃te]: 782
montre [mɔ̃tʁ]: 247, 500
montréal [mɔ̃ʁeal]: 784
mort [mɔʁ]: 585
morte [mɔʁt]: 984, 984
mot [mo]: 379, 407

musée [myze]: 295

musique [myzik]: 30, 196, 344, 384, 385, 477

n'a [n̪a]: 342, 488, 489, 504, 507, 515, 521, 523, 622, 711, 781, 796

n'achète [n̪aʃɛt]: 553

nage [naʒ]: 177

nageait [naʒɛ]: 667

nager [naʒe]: 758, 956

nageur [naʒœʁ]: 43

n'ai [n̪ɛ]: 12, 42, 105, 486, 502, 512, 526, 608, 611, 612, 618, 650, 662, 761, 798, 799, 900, 914, 945

n'aimais [n̪ɛmɛ]: 751

n'aime [n̪ɛm]: 319, 328, 329, 333, 345, 348, 351, 355, 358, 367, 480

n'aiment [n̪ɛm]: 347

n'allait [n̪alɛ]: 695

n'arrive [n̪aʁiv]: 897

n'as [n̪a]: 503

n'avait [n̪avɛ]: 621

n'avons [n̪avɔ̃]: 528, 613, 734, 925

ne [nø]: 2, 14, 16, 32, 37, 40, 44, 91, 151, 153, 154, 157, 162, 165, 168, 190, 191, 193, 195, 197... +112

n'écoutais [n̪ekute]: 669

neige [nɛʒ]: 191

neige-t-il [nɛʒ t̪il]: 408

n'en [n̪ɑ̃]: 248, 494, 495, 496, 498, 499, 732

n'est [n̪e]: 17, 34, 38, 74, 159, 182, 186, 189, 371, 517, 616, 730, 913, 951, 970, 973, 983

n'étaient [n̪ete]: 538

n'étais [n̪ete]: 562, 664

n'étais-tu [n̪ete ty]: 664

n'était [n̪ete]: 530, 557, 558, 657, 666, 990

n'étions [n̪etjɔ̃]: 541, 557

nettoyait [netwajɛ]: 687

neuf [nœ]: 294, 430, 575, 638, 687, 713, 860

neuf [nœf]: 570, 688, 833

neuves [nœv]: 61

new [nuw]: 22, 263, 380, 797, 993

noir [nwaʁ]: 103, 155

noire [nwaʁ]: 95

noires [nwaʁ]: 132

nom [nɔ̃]: 147, 308, 807

nombreux [nɔ̃bʁø]: 965

non [nɔ̃]: 16, 48, 54, 56, 58, 85, 91, 95, 97, 105, 136, 140, 144, 151, 153, 154, 216, 220, 222, 226... +51

n'ont [n̪ɔ̃]: 327, 487, 509, 518, 954

normalement [nɔʁmal°mɑ̃]: 771

nos [no]: 274, 584, 606, 955

note [nɔt]: 586

notre [nɔtʁ]: 483, 557, 950, 955

n'oublie [n̪ubli]: 940

nourriture [nuʁityʁ]: 299

nous [nu]: 161, 167, 173, 178, 274, 278, 291, 302, 310, 323, 341, 365, 511, 528, 541, 557, 572... +60

nouveau [nuvo]: 508, 554, 853, 863, 936, 942, 943, 957, 976

nouveaux [nuvo]: 658, 958

nouvel [nuvɛ]: 180, 953, 979

nouvelle [nuvɛ]: 950

nouvelle [nuvɛl]: 566, 899, 906, 910, 911, 924, 934, 937

nouvelles [nuvɛl]: 131, 359, 472, 684, 912

nouvelle-zélande [nuvɛl zeland]: 812

nuit [nɥi]: 292, 740

numéro [nymeʁo]: 75, 340, 512

n'y [n̪i]: 371, 548, 561, 773, 994

occupée [okype]: 725

oiseaux [z̪wazo]: 674

on [ɔ̃]: 224, 511, 573, 576, 651

ont [ɔ̃]: 123, 485, 516, 524, 617, 619, 724, 811

ont [l̪ɔ̃]: 506, 617, 916

ont-elles [ɔ̃ t̪ɛl]: 544

onze [ɔ̃z]: 552, 668, 707

orange [oʁɑ̃ʒ]: 604

oranges [z̪oʁɑ̃ʒ]: 125

ordinateur [l̪ɔʁdinatœʁ]: 953

ordinateur [n̪ɔʁdinatœʁ]: 497, 966

où [p̪u]: 415

où [u]: 63, 78, 92, 121, 166, 179, 210, 234, 240, 368, 377, 398, 461, 468, 520, 535, 552, 556, 561, 562... +12

ou [u]: 902

où [z_u]: 776

oublies [ubli]: 447

oui [wi]: 52, 60, 62, 83, 87, 89, 99, 142, 152, 155, 156, 201, 203, 214, 218, 224, 228, 254, 424, 497... +19

ouvert [uvɛ]: 661

ouvert [uvɛʁ]: 579

ouvertes [uvɛʁt]: 559

ouverts [uvɛʁ]: 113

ouvrent [uvʁ]: 294

ouvrir [z_uvʁiʁ]: 526

pantalon [pɑ̃talɔ̃]: 658, 672

papier [papje]: 621

paquet [pakɛ]: 466

par [pa]: 762

par [paʁ]: 292, 759

parapluie [paʁaplɥi]: 203, 427, 510, 697

parc [paʁk]: 166, 681

parce [paʁs]: 558, 567, 946, 948

pardon [paʁdɔ̃]: 460

parents [paʁɑ̃]: 57, 70, 111, 240, 241, 264, 377, 386, 398, 617

parfois [paʁfwa]: 280, 332, 359, 382, 406, 414, 767

parle [paʁl]: 293, 335, 366, 369

parlé [paʁle]: 573, 944

parlent [paʁl]: 386

parler [paʁle]: 474, 724, 948, 952

parles [paʁl]: 269, 393

parle-t-il [paʁl t_il]: 393

parlez-vous [paʁle vu]: 460

pars [paʁ]: 213, 214, 223, 933

part [paʁ]: 919

parti [paʁti]: 864, 941

partie [paʁti]: 709, 733

partir [paʁtiʁ]: 928, 992

partout [paʁtu]: 515, 804

pas [pa]: 2, 12, 14, 16, 17, 32, 34, 37, 38, 40, 42, 44, 74, 91, 105, 151, 153, 154, 157, 159... +201

passé [pase]: 538, 951, 997

passeport [paspɔʁ]: 787, 897

patron [patʁɔ̃]: 77

pattes [pat]: 527

payé [peje]: 586, 925, 959

payer [peje]: 959

pays [pei]: 36, 873, 991

peignait [pɛɲɛ]: 718

peintre [pɛ̃tʁ]: 1000

pendant [pɑ̃dɑ̃]: 711, 974

pense [pɑ̃s]: 282

perd [pɛʁ]: 600

perdu [pɛʁdy]: 600, 641, 740, 787, 897, 907, 908, 909, 918

perdue [pɛʁdy]: 904

père [pɛʁ]: 80, 130, 387, 476, 513, 944

pérou [peʁu]: 790

personne [pɛʁsɔn]: 369, 775, 875, 954

petit [p°ti]: 173, 337, 411, 596, 686, 728

petite [p°tit]: 557

peu [pø]: 60, 622

peur [pøʁ]: 540

peut [pø]: 946, 949

peux [pø]: 167, 222, 428, 477, 526, 947, 948

peux-tu [pø ty]: 474

photo [foto]: 129, 372, 449

photos [foto]: 448

piano [pjano]: 186, 287, 338, 339, 416, 750, 894

pièce [pjɛs]: 578, 579, 661

pièces [pjɛs]: 965, 972

pied [pje]: 176, 280

piscine [pisin]: 667

plage [plaʒ]: 178, 651

plaît [plɛ]: 164, 227, 425

pleures-tu [plœʁ ty]: 236

pleut [plø]: 165, 194, 202, 251, 252, 265, 325, 415, 427, 432, 464, 832, 890

pleut-il [plø t_il]: 225, 844

pleuvait [pløvɛ]: 670, 676, 712, 714

pleuvait-il [pløvɛ t_il]: 690

plu   [ply]: 571, 583, 615, 659, 711, 832
pluie   [plɥi]: 464, 571
plupart   [plypaʀ]: 524, 767
plus   [ply]: 916
plus   [plys]: 167, 474, 597, 626, 746, 749, 903
plusieurs   [plyzjœ]: 775, 801, 875, 993
plusieurs   [plyzjœʀ]: 505, 762, 795, 800, 965, 972, 986, 991, 1000
poème   [poɛm]: 809
poèmes   [poɛm]: 965, 972
police   [polis]: 731
politique   [politik]: 44, 363
pomme   [pɔm]: 169
portable   [pɔʀtabl]: 490
portais   [pɔʀtɛ]: 756
portait   [pɔʀtɛ]: 672, 693, 699, 737
portait-il   [pɔʀte t il]: 692
porte   [pɔʀt]: 188, 198, 248, 311, 362, 526, 672
porté   [pɔʀte]: 979
portée   [pɔʀte]: 934, 937
portefeuille   [pɔʀtˤfœj]: 918
portes   [pɔʀt]: 483
portes-tu   [pɔʀt ty]: 204, 247
postales   [pɔstal]: 72
poste   [pɔst]: 116, 620, 950
pour   [pu]: 395, 900
pour   [puʀ]: 380, 401, 411, 721, 723, 724, 877, 878, 879, 880, 881, 955, 1000
pourquoi   [puʀkwa]: 74, 118, 204, 236, 238, 243, 429, 462, 545, 563, 567, 664, 691, 692
pratiques-tu   [pʀatik ty]: 764
préfère   [pʀefɛʀ]: 480
préféré   [pʀefeʀe]: 813
préférée   [pʀefeʀe]: 27, 28
préfères   [pʀefɛʀ]: 441
prenait   [pʀønɛ]: 686, 728
prend   [pʀɑ̃]: 179, 337, 426, 431, 468
prend-il   [pʀɑ̃ d il]: 448
prendre   [pʀɑ̃dʀ]: 449, 723
prends   [pʀɑ̃]: 203, 427
prenons   [pʀˤnɔ̃]: 173

préparait   [pʀepaʀɛ]: 685
près   [pʀɛ]: 116, 365, 375, 391, 770
présenter   [pʀezɑ̃te]: 902
principale   [pʀɛ̃sipal]: 835
pris   [pʀi]: 596, 598, 605, 630, 923
prix   [pʀi]: 1000
problèmes   [pʀoblɛm]: 517
prochaine   [pʀoʃɛn]: 936
promenade   [pʀomnad]: 681
promenait   [pʀomˤnɛ]: 700
promener   [pʀomne]: 356
promènes-tu   [pʀomɛn ty]: 414
propre   [pʀɔpʀ]: 557, 895
puis-je   [pɥi ʒø]: 550
qu'anabel   [k (...)]: 560
quand   [kɑ̃]: 595, 676, 690, 701, 710, 712, 714, 725, 731, 735, 745, 751, 768, 817, 821, 822, 839, 840, 843, 844... +12
quarante-cinq   [kaʀɑ̃tsɛ̃k]: 682, 683
qu'as-tu   [k a ty]: 705, 964
qu'a-t-il   [k a t il]: 669, 703
quatorze   [katɔʀz]: 689, 713, 981
quatre   [katʀ]: 293, 366, 483, 524, 597
quatre-vingt-dix   [katʀˤvɛ̃di]: 585
quatre-vingt-dix-huit   [katʀˤvɛ̃dizɥi]: 13
quatre-vingt-dix-neuf   [katʀˤvɛ̃diznœf]: 688, 833
quatre-vingt-quinze   [katʀˤvɛ̃kɛ̃z]: 570
que   [kø]: 206, 208, 215, 233, 235, 242, 244, 255, 375, 379, 382, 383, 386, 387, 388, 401, 403, 404, 407, 411... +37
quel   [kɛ]: 23, 25, 49, 68, 75, 123, 127, 137, 147, 149, 405
qu'elle   [k ɛl]: 609, 610, 946
quelle   [kɛ]: 27, 409, 476, 637, 727, 929, 938, 941, 967, 982, 988
quelle   [kɛl]: 66, 102, 131, 378, 400, 408, 472, 492, 731
quelque   [kɛlk]: 249, 478, 519, 550, 919
quelques   [kɛl]: 750, 763, 770
quelques   [kɛlk]: 556, 724, 789, 834, 885
quelqu'un   [kɛlkœ̃]: 177, 470

quels [kɛl]: 29, 772
qu'emily [k (...)]: 376
qu'est-ce [kɛs°]: 233, 235, 237, 242, 379, 401, 407, 429, 441, 444, 462, 493, 519, 999
qu'eveline [k (...)]: 616
qui [ki]: 76, 108, 129, 211, 462, 519, 783
qu'il [k‿il]: 202, 251, 415, 558, 652, 718, 728, 837, 894, 948
qu'ils [k‿il]: 237, 457, 954
quinze [kɛ̃z]: 580, 594, 677, 686, 871
qu'isidor [k (...)]: 932
quitté [kite]: 594
quoi [kwa]: 29, 443, 463
qu'oliver [k (...)]: 905
rappeler [ʁap°le]: 167
reçois [ʁ°swa]: 359
regardais-tu [ʁ°gaʁdɛ ty]: 710
regardait [ʁ°gaʁdɛ]: 667
regarde [ʁ°gaʁd]: 5, 168, 183, 246, 309, 312, 353, 354, 412, 417, 428, 433, 469, 607, 769, 830, 831
regardé [ʁ°gaʁde]: 608, 623, 628, 709
regardent [ʁ°gaʁd]: 209, 237, 257, 361
regardent-ils [ʁ°gaʁ d‿il]: 241
regarder [ʁ°gaʁde]: 157, 665, 769, 946
regardes-tu [ʁ°gaʁd ty]: 221, 243, 245, 400, 412
regarde-t-il [ʁ°gaʁd t‿il]: 830
regardons [ʁ°gaʁdɔ̃]: 323
remy [ʁ°mi]: 892
rencontre [ʁɑ̃kɔ̃tʁ]: 297
rencontré [ʁɑ̃kɔ̃tʁe]: 722, 806, 810, 902, 958, 989
rencontrés [ʁɑ̃kɔ̃tʁe]: 931
rend [ʁɑ̃]: 276, 479, 515, 599
rends [ʁɑ̃]: 315, 316
renée [ʁ°ne]: 898
rentrait [ʁɑ̃tʁɛ]: 698
rentre [ʁɑ̃tʁ]: 475
rentré [ʁɑ̃tʁe]: 905, 913, 968
rentrées [ʁɑ̃tʁe]: 645
rentrer [ʁɑ̃tʁe]: 471, 948
rentrés [ʁɑ̃tʁe]: 645

répondu [ʁepɔ̃dy]: 704
réponse [ʁepɔ̃s]: 437, 447
restaurant [ʁɛstoʁɑ̃]: 357
resté [ʁɛste]: 964
restées [ʁɛste]: 660
restés [ʁɛste]: 660
retard [ʁ°taʁ]: 16, 53, 98, 118, 332, 537, 545, 546, 563, 567, 636, 800, 849, 874
réunion [ʁeynjɔ̃]: 636, 664
réveillé [ʁeveje]: 673
riche [ʁiʃ]: 2
ris-tu [ʁi ty]: 462
rit [ʁi]: 187
rit-il [ʁi t‿il]: 238
rivière [ʁivjɛʁ]: 177
robe [ʁɔb]: 934, 937
rock [ʁɔk]: 346
roll [ʁɔl]: 346
romantiques [ʁomɑ̃tik]: 352
roues [ʁu]: 524
rouge [ʁuʒ]: 67
rue [ʁy]: 722, 748, 835
sa [sa]: 7, 298, 595, 679, 682, 718, 825, 895, 916, 960
sac [sak]: 3, 93, 102, 493, 590, 694, 723
sacs [sak]: 4
sais [sɛ]: 368, 461, 520, 556, 561, 656, 669, 783, 994
sait-il [sɛ t‿il]: 933
sale [sal]: 298, 895
salle [sal]: 79
salut [saly]: 181
sans [sɑ̃]: 923
s'appelle [s‿apɛl]: 148
s'apprêtent [s‿apʁɛt]: 896
satisfaits [satisfɛ]: 557
savoir [savwaʁ]: 437
se [sø]: 224, 276, 356, 479, 484, 515, 599, 605, 700, 883, 898, 954
seize [sɛz]: 666, 713
séjourné [seʒuʁne]: 584, 634, 635
séjournent [seʒuʁn]: 220

séjournent-ils [seʒuʁ n‿il]: 219
séjourner [seʒuʁne]: 364
séjournions [seʒuʁnjɔ̃]: 178
semaine [sᵊmɛn]: 536, 558, 565, 568, 577, 587, 600, 717, 759, 879, 908, 911, 936, 976
semaines [sᵊmɛn]: 863
sens [sɑ̃s]: 201, 255, 256, 522, 551, 956
sens-tu [sɑ̃s ty]: 200
sent [sɑ̃]: 484
sept [sɛ]: 271, 292, 314, 594, 629, 686, 771, 872, 894
sept [sɛt]: 124
serveur [sɛʁvœʁ]: 766
ses [se]: 8, 264, 361, 392, 600, 601, 721, 946, 958, 1000
s'est [s‿e]: 578, 593, 595, 656, 716, 717, 837, 915, 921
s'est-elle [s‿e t‿ɛl]: 655
seul [sœl]: 304
seule [sœl]: 304
seulement [sœlᵊmɑ̃]: 930
si [si]: 74, 462, 691, 957, 959
siège [sjɛʒ]: 90, 473
signifie [siɲifi]: 379, 407
s'il [s‿il]: 164, 425, 497, 498, 499, 500, 501, 958, 960
silence [silɑ̃s]: 164, 425
silencieuse [silɑ̃sjøz]: 369
silencieux [silɑ̃sjø]: 164
six [si]: 593, 974
six [sis]: 485, 527, 838, 857, 886, 892
ski [ski]: 128
sœur [sœʁ]: 10, 109, 388, 405, 463, 781, 952
sœurs [sœʁ]: 482, 501, 505
soif [swaf]: 12, 85, 152
soir [swaʁ]: 530, 534, 551, 562, 572, 601, 610, 623, 627, 649, 675, 709, 736, 964, 980, 985, 988
soirée [swaʁe]: 312
soirs [swaʁ]: 601, 759, 769
sois [swa]: 164
sol [sɔl]: 172, 184, 253

soleil [solɛj]: 197, 217, 273, 674
sommes [sɔm]: 6, 167, 178, 302, 603, 613, 620, 633, 645, 651, 657, 660, 670, 676, 714, 774, 847, 848... +3
son [sɔ̃]: 147, 319, 336, 370, 578, 596, 598, 807, 850, 863, 872, 936, 942, 943, 957, 959
sonne [sɔn]: 160
sonné [sone]: 701, 703
sont [sɔ̃]: 4, 8, 14, 29, 35, 37, 58, 61, 62, 72, 73, 88, 89, 131, 132, 154, 163, 166, 457... +24
sont-elles [sɔ̃ t‿ɛl]: 61, 72, 154
sont-ils [sɔ̃ t‿il]: 57, 113, 117, 839
sors-tu [sɔʁ ty]: 759
sort [sɔʁ]: 609
sorte [sɔʁt]: 492
sorti [sɔʁti]: 967, 978
sortie [sɔʁti]: 610, 983
sorties [sɔʁti]: 670, 676, 714, 896
sortir [sɔʁtiʁ]: 464, 759, 896, 949
sortis [sɔʁti]: 670, 676, 714, 896
sous [su]: 429, 464
souvent [suvɑ̃]: 278, 280, 291, 308, 314, 323, 325, 332, 334, 354, 355, 360, 365, 395, 412, 414, 420, 433... +11
souviens [suvjɛ̃]: 776, 807
souviens-tu [suvjɛ̃ ty]: 439
sport [spɔʁ]: 115, 127, 128, 758, 764
stylo [stilo]: 621
sud [syd]: 786
suis [sɥi]: 2, 9, 16, 26, 39, 40, 48, 52, 83, 136, 140, 142, 151, 156, 157, 176, 190, 192... +25
suis-je [sɥi ʒø]: 53, 98
super [sypɛʁ]: 653
supermarché [sypɛʁmaʁʃe]: 678, 744
sur [sy]: 192
sur [syʁ]: 129, 172, 176, 178, 184, 253, 514, 561, 590, 748, 835
survenu [syʁvᵊny]: 582
t'a [t‿a]: 731
ta [ta]: 27, 55, 59, 63, 66, 94, 110, 143, 388, 405, 463, 566, 826, 904, 952, 999

table [tabl]: 174, 429, 561, 590

tableaux [tablo]: 1000

t'ai [t_ɛ]: 710

taïwan [taiwan]: 994

tante [tãt]: 871

t'appelle [t_apɛl]: 382

t'appelles-tu [t_apɛl ty]: 19, 45, 133

tard [taʁ]: 167, 475, 597

tas [ta]: 803, 806, 811

tasse [tas]: 593

taxi [taksi]: 9, 232, 598, 645, 754

te [tø]: 164, 167, 200, 227, 255, 378, 399, 414, 439, 446

télé [tele]: 157, 168, 183, 209, 221, 241, 245, 309, 312, 323, 353, 354, 400, 412, 417, 428, 433, 469, 607... +13

téléphone [telefɔn]: 75, 160, 340, 499, 512, 520, 591, 701, 703, 704, 959

temps [tã]: 274, 404, 528, 549, 612, 662, 761, 767, 824, 826, 828, 830, 841, 842, 990, 997, 998

tennis [tenis]: 6, 279, 290, 349, 376, 390, 392, 467, 611, 639, 683, 707, 708, 763, 798, 987

terminal [teʁminal]: 595

terre [tɛʁ]: 273

t'es [t_ɛ]: 690, 947

tes [te]: 29, 57, 61, 70, 88, 111, 117, 119, 123, 131, 154, 219, 240, 241, 375, 377, 386, 398, 404, 544... +4

t'es-tu [t_ɛ ty]: 792

tête [tɛt]: 484, 522, 837

thé [te]: 320, 321, 480

théâtre [teatʁ]: 965, 972

t'intéresses-tu [t_ẽteʁɛs ty]: 29, 115

toi [twa]: 389, 390, 394, 396, 440, 514, 623, 624, 625, 626, 627

tombé [tɔ̃be]: 719

ton [tɔ̃]: 18, 25, 75, 78, 80, 86, 93, 102, 112, 127, 268, 387, 393, 403, 476, 490, 493, 512, 513... +12

tôt [to]: 276, 277, 303, 399, 575, 626, 673, 771

toujours [tuʒuʁ]: 276, 277, 303, 305, 307, 311, 315, 317, 357, 399, 599, 605, 935

tourne [tuʁn]: 273

tous [tu]: 266, 343, 356, 359, 381, 394, 394, 430, 431, 569, 601, 602, 604, 758, 769, 811

tout [tu]: 525, 927, 970

toute [tut]: 571, 583, 825, 832

train [tʁẽ]: 157, 158, 159, 163, 167, 182, 186, 189, 190, 193, 195, 199, 249, 358, 449, 451, 455, 457, 478... +7

transportait [tʁãspɔʁtɛ]: 694, 697, 723

travail [tʁavaj]: 17, 112, 276, 277, 280, 297, 315, 319, 336, 367, 463, 479, 489, 508, 511, 529, 530, 547, 558... +22

travaillais [tʁavajɛ]: 675

travaillais-tu [tʁavajɛ ty]: 668

travaillait [tʁavajɛ]: 743

travaille [tʁavaj]: 164, 215, 216, 261, 262, 270, 305, 387, 405, 425, 430, 744, 836, 850

travaillé [tʁavaje]: 570, 576, 619, 622

travailler [tʁavaje]: 157, 476, 713

travailles [tʁavaj]: 322, 397

travailles-tu [tʁavaj ty]: 374

travaille-t-elle [tʁavaj t_ɛl]: 397

travaillons [tʁavajɔ̃]: 341

trente [tʁãt]: 126, 271, 310, 430, 575, 632, 638, 647, 668, 675, 687, 706, 707, 713

trente-trois [tʁãttʁwa]: 138

très [tʁɛ]: 13, 14, 36, 74, 81, 269, 270, 275, 288, 297, 298, 305, 322, 323, 325, 334, 336, 338, 339, 341... +29

trois [tʁwa]: 485, 516, 577, 759, 805, 819, 854, 855, 863, 868, 870, 877, 888, 893, 912

trouver [tʁuve]: 897

tu [ty]: 16, 54, 99, 162, 176, 213, 222, 223, 231, 233, 235, 255, 269, 322, 343, 391, 393, 397, 401, 415... +23

un [d_œ̃]: 170

un   [œ̃]: 60, 188, 204, 232, 380, 410,
      451, 452, 486, 497, 498, 499, 501,
      508, 510, 527, 540, 570, 581... +19
un   [ʁ‿œ̃]: 945, 956
un   [t‿œ̃]: 13, 36, 73, 185, 467, 485,
      559, 617, 621, 672, 680, 694, 699,
      702, 723, 737, 750, 757, 791... +7
un   [z‿œ̃]: 178, 180, 203, 231, 261, 427,
      596, 598, 744, 772, 850
une   [d‿yn]: 179, 426, 431, 468
une   [ʁ‿yn]: 192, 455, 661
une   [t‿yn]: 369, 372, 488, 523, 583,
      681, 775, 917
une   [yn]: 169, 189, 247, 360, 419, 449,
      490, 491, 494, 495, 496, 500, 513,
      593, 604, 672... +20
une   [z‿yn]: 262, 288, 413, 570, 605,
      630, 743, 765, 836, 880, 890, 899
usine   [yzin]: 743
va   [va]: 80, 81, 106, 107, 519, 558
vacances   [vakãs]: 178, 543, 565, 584,
      625, 642, 711, 815, 881, 901, 963,
      996
vacantes   [vakãt]: 875
vais   [vɛ]: 181, 280, 304, 767
valises   [valiz]: 955
vas-tu   [va ty]: 406, 409, 767
va-t-elle   [va t‿ɛl]: 210, 234
va-t-il   [va t‿il]: 941
vécu   [veky]: 775, 825, 842, 974, 993
végétarien   [veʒetaʁjɛ̃]: 373
vélo   [velo]: 356, 414, 486, 504, 515,
      700, 923
vendre   [vãdʁ]: 960
vendredi   [vãdʁ°di]: 552, 606, 977
vendu   [vãdy]: 750, 960
vendue   [vãdy]: 765
venir   [v°niʁ]: 752
venteux   [vãtø]: 33, 34
venue   [v°ny]: 616
venues   [v°ny]: 606
venus   [v°ny]: 606
veston   [vɛstɔ̃]: 554, 693, 737
vêtements   [vɛt°mã]: 311, 658
veulent   [vœl]: 939

veut   [vø]: 471, 521
veux   [vø]: 396, 401, 444, 464, 814
veux-tu   [vø ty]: 396, 437
viande   [vjãd]: 373, 768
vie   [vi]: 825, 866
vieil   [vjɛj]: 13
viennent   [vjɛn]: 606, 926
viennent-ils   [vjɛ n‿il]: 929
viens   [vjɛ̃]: 22, 65, 927, 945, 952, 956
viens-tu   [vjɛ̃ ty]: 21, 64, 114, 465, 475
vient   [vjɛ̃]: 100, 101, 146, 915, 928,
      948, 949
vient-elle   [vjɛ̃ t‿ɛl]: 145
vieux   [vjø]: 681
ville   [vil]: 413
villes   [vil]: 267
vingt   [vɛ̃]: 24, 272, 813, 873, 874, 882,
      883, 930
vingt-cinq   [vɛ̃tsɛ̃]: 50
vingt-deux   [vɛ̃tdø]: 539, 580, 632
vingt-quatre   [vɛ̃katʁ]: 69
vingt-six   [vɛ̃tsi]: 150
vingt-trois   [vɛ̃ttʁwa]: 539
vis   [vis]: 413, 861, 862, 993
visité   [vizite]: 991
visitée   [vizite]: 587
vis-tu   [vis ty]: 413, 852
vit   [vi]: 263, 824, 846, 871, 875
vite   [vit]: 691, 732, 903
vit-elle   [vi t‿ɛl]: 824
vitesse   [vitɛs]: 731
vitre   [vitʁ]: 455, 735
vitres   [vitʁ]: 454
vivent   [viv]: 288, 375, 377, 916
vivions   [vivjɔ̃]: 671, 770
vivons   [vivɔ̃]: 835, 974
voici   [vwasi]: 18, 931, 937
voilà   [vwala]: 5
voir   [vwaʁ]: 606, 721, 725, 749, 939
voisins   [vwazɛ̃]: 958
voit   [vwa]: 224, 601

voiture [vwatyʁ]: 66, 94, 298, 331,
    333, 342, 360, 479, 483, 486, 491,
    492, 496, 513, 515, 595, 599, 679...
    +16
voitures [vwatyʁ]: 524, 912
vol [vɔl]: 380, 596
vole [vɔl]: 283
volé [vole]: 592, 788, 796
vont [võ]: 70, 71, 111, 119, 120, 240
voulais [vulɛ]: 581
vous [vu]: 425, 473, 902
voyage [vwajaʒ]: 395, 541, 617, 955,
    991
voyagé [vwajaʒe]: 781, 804, 814
voyager [vwajaʒe]: 358, 762, 814
voyages-tu [vwajaʒ ty]: 762
voyage-t-il [vwajaʒ t il]: 395
voyons [vwajõ]: 365, 749

vrai [vʁɛ]: 371
vraiment [vʁɛmã]: 228
vu [vy]: 614, 618, 736, 776, 783, 807,
    813, 919, 939, 961, 980, 980
vues [vy]: 601, 715
vus [vy]: 601, 715
week-ends [wikɛnd]: 278, 383, 434,
    603
y [i]: 560, 812
y [l i]: 547, 556, 750, 763, 770, 863,
    864, 865, 866, 868, 872, 877, 878,
    881, 883, 884, 885, 975, 984, 996
yeux [z jø]: 481
yoga [joga]: 394
york [jɔʁk]: 22, 263, 380, 797, 993